Stanislav and Christina Grof

beyond death

The gates of consciousness

with 158 illustrations, 17 in color

Thames and Hudson

Dedicated with love
to Than and Sarah

ART AND IMAGINATION
General Editor: Jill Purce

First published in the United States of America in
1980 by Thames and Hudson Inc., 500 Fifth Avenue,
New York, New York 10110
Reprinted 1995

Library of Congress Catalog Card Number 79-67540
ISBN 0-500-81019-2

Printed and bound in Singapore

Contents

The gates of consciousness

Plates   33

Themes   65

Bibliography and acknowledgments   96

The gates of consciousness

Ancient wisdom and modern science

The central theme of the medieval literature on the art of dying was expressed succinctly in the Latin phrase, *Mors certa, hora incerta*: the most certain thing in life is that we will die; the least certain is the time when it will happen. And the medieval philosopher would add that because of this utter uncertainty about the timing of death, we should be prepared for it at all times.

The recognition of the utmost importance of dying as an integral aspect of life is characteristic of all ancient and non-Western cultures, where the theme of death has had a deep influence on religion, ritual life, mythology, art and philosophy. Awareness of the significance of death was similarly a part of Western civilization until the time of the Industrial Revolution. One of the tolls that Westerners have had to pay for rapid technological progress is profound alienation from the fundamental biological aspects of existence. This process has found its most drastic expression in relation to the basic triad of life – birth, sex and death. The psychological revolution initiated by Sigmund Freud has to a great extent lifted the repression imposed on human sexuality. In the last decade, we have been witnessing a comparable development in the areas of death and birth. This process has been manifest not only in rapid development of insights into the significance of the experience of birth and death, but also in revolutionary changes in the medical practices concerning childbirth and in the treatment of the dying.

It is not accidental that the lifting of the taboos related to birth and death has been accompanied by rediscovery of spirituality that had also been one of the victims of the rapid progress of materialistic science. As modern knowledge of these areas advances, it is becoming increasingly clear that birth, sex, death and spirituality are intimately interwoven, and have powerful representations in the human unconscious. Since this insight represents an essential part of many ancient cosmologies, religions and philosophies, the new discoveries are rapidly bridging the gap between ancient wisdom and modern science. In the recent process of convergence of modern physics, consciousness research and mysticism,* many ancient systems of knowledge previously regarded as obsolete curiosities are found to be of extraordinary relevance for our everyday life. This is certainly true of ancient knowledge concerning death and dying, such as eschatological mythologies, shamanic practices, the 'books of the dead' and death-rebirth mysteries.

*The interested reader will find a detailed discussion of the convergence of the Oriental mystical systems and quantum-relativistic physics in Fritjof Capra's *The Tao of Physics* (see Bibliography).

In order to appreciate the nature and scope of the present revolution concerning death and dying, it is necessary to realize the degree of dehumanization and alienation that technological development has brought to the West.

The belief in an afterlife is part of our religious tradition, but for the sophisticated Westerner, religion has lost much of its original significance and vitality. Non-Western cultures have retained the original power of cosmologies, religious systems and philosophies in which death is not seen as the absolute and irrevocable end of existence, and consciousness or life in some form continues beyond the point of biological demise. Their concepts of the afterlife cover an extremely wide range, from sequences of highly abstract states of consciousness to images of an otherworld resembling earthly existence; but in all these beliefs, death is regarded as transition or transfiguration and not as the final annihilation of the individual.

Eschatological mythologies not only give detailed descriptions of the afterlife states of mind or abodes of the deceased, such as heaven, paradise or hell, but offer precise cartographies to guide the dying through the sequential changes of consciousness that occur during the critical period of transition.

Such belief systems certainly have the power to alleviate the fear of death, and in their extreme forms may even reverse the values assigned to living and dying. For the Hindu, unenlightened life appears to be a state of separation, imprisonment and delusion, whereas death is reunion, spiritual liberation and awakening. Death represents an opportunity for the individual self (jiva) to break away from worldly illusion (maya) and experience its divine nature (Atman-Brahman). In systems in which reincarnation plays an important role, such as Hinduism, Buddhism, Jainism and Tibetan Tantrism, dying can be seen as more important than living. Knowledge of, and the right attitude towards, the experiences associated with dying can have a critical influence on the future incarnation. For the Buddhist, suffering is intrinsic to biological existence, and the ultimate spiritual goal is to extinguish the fire of life and leave the wheel of death and rebirth, the chain of repeated incarnations.

Dying is sometimes seen as a step up in the spiritual or cosmological hierarchy, a promotion into the world of revered ancestors, powerful spirits or demigods, or as a transition from the complicated earthly life fraught with suffering and problems to a blissful existence in the solar region or the realms of gods. More frequently the concept of afterlife involves dichotomies and polarities; there are hells and purgatories as well as celestial realms and paradisiacal states. The posthumous journey of the soul is understood as a complex and difficult one. It is therefore essential to be well prepared when death comes. At the very least, it is necessary to acquire a knowledge of the cartography and laws of the afterlife existence.

Many traditions include the belief that one can do more to prepare for death than just acquire intellectual knowledge of the process of dying. Mind-altering technologies have been developed using psychedelic substances or powerful non-drug methods that make possible real experiential training for dying. In this context, compelling psychological encounters with death, so profound and shattering as to be indistinguishable from actual biological annihilation, are followed by the sense of spiritual rebirth. This is the core-experience of shamanic initiation, rites of passage and mystery religions. Symbolic death of this kind not only gives a deep realization of the impermanence of biological existence, but facilitates spiritual opening, and provides insight into the transcendent nature of human consciousness.

Literary documents known as the 'books of the dead' offer precise and detailed guidance for the dying. The most famous of these 'books' are the Egyptian *Pert em hru* and the Tibetan *Bardo Thödol*, but similar texts exist in the Hindu, Moslem and Mesoamerican traditions. The European counterpart of these books is a vast body of medieval literature known as *Ars Moriendi* or *The Art of Dying*. Since the states of mind associated with dying can be experienced during life, these texts can also be used as manuals for meditation or initiation.

The individual dying in an ancient or pre-industrial culture is thus equipped with a religious or philosophical system that transcends death, and is likely to have had considerable experiential training in altered states of consciousness, including symbolic confrontations with death. The approach of death is faced in the nourishing context of the extended family, clan, or tribe, and with its support – sometimes even with specific and expert guidance through the successive stages of dying.

The situation of an average Westerner facing death is in sharp contrast to the above in every respect. The teachings of religion about the afterlife have been misinterpreted as historical and geographical references, and in this form discredited by materialistic science. Religion has become to a large extent externalized, and has lost connection with its original experiential sources. The educated Westerner tends to consider belief in consciousness after death and in the posthumous journey of the soul as manifestations of the primitive fears and magical thinking of people who have been denied the privilege of scientific knowledge. In the Cartesian-Newtonian worldview, consciousness is the product of the brain and, as such, ceases at the time of physical death. Although there are disagreements about whether death should be defined as cessation of heart-beat or extinction of electrical brain activity, the idea of consciousness after death is incompatible with materialistic science.

In the context of our pragmatic philosophy emphasizing success and achievement, aging and dying are not seen as integral parts of the life-process, but as defeat and a painful reminder of the limits of our ability to control nature. The terminally ill and dying are seen in our culture as losers, and tend to see themselves as such.

Contemporary medicine has been indulging in technological wizardry and over-specialized body mechanics, and has lost the holistic point of view characteristic of healing. Its approach to the dying is dominated by a determined effort to conquer death and delay its advent at all cost. In this struggle for mechanical prolongation of life, very little attention is paid to the quality of the patient's remaining days, or to his psychological, philosophical and spiritual needs. There is a tendency to remove the elderly and dying from the family and everyday life and place them in nursing homes and hospitals, where meaningful human contact is replaced by sophisticated gadgetry – oxygen tents, infusion bottles and tubes, electric pacemakers, and monitors of vital functions.

Not only do contemporary religion, philosophy, social structure and medical science have little to offer to ease the mental suffering of the dying, but until quite recently even psychologists and psychiatrists participated in the massive denial and repression surrounding death. The confrontation with death – the ultimate biological, emotional, psychological, philosophical and spiritual crisis – was probably the only area of life where expert psychological help was not available. Mental health professionals studied a variety of relatively insignificant problems with pedantic attention to detail, systematically avoiding investigation of the experiential world of the dying.

Although the present situation is still far from ideal, during the last decade there have been dramatic changes in the awareness and attitudes of those concerned with the dying. This progress was largely initiated by the work of the Swiss-born American psychiatrist Elisabeth Kübler-Ross and her pioneering book *On Death and Dying*. In addition to her world-wide efforts to alleviate the emotional suffering of the dying, Dr Kübler-Ross created positive interest in the experiences associated with death. Another important avenue of thanatological research has developed independently, in psychedelic therapy with cancer patients. It has been shown* that LSD experiences of death and rebirth and mystical states of consciousness can change patients' concepts of death and life and alleviate their fears of dying. Psychedelic therapy has proved to be more than an important tool in the control of mental and physical pain, it has contributed greatly to our understanding of the experience of death. The findings of these modern studies of death and dying have in general confirmed to a great extent the claims of eschatological systems of non-Western cultures, and have generated in the West a new respect for ancient and Oriental religions and philosophies. It has become increasingly clear that these systems of belief reflect profound understanding of the human mind and of unusual states of consciousness, embodying knowledge that deals with the most universal aspect of human existence, and thus is highly relevant for all of us.

* For detailed discussion of these experiments, see Stanislav Grof and Joan Halifax, *The Human Encounter with Death* (see Bibliography).

Experiences of clinical death and near-death

When in the past Western science dismissed the concept of consciousness after death as a fabrication based on wishful thinking and superstition, this judgment was not based on the careful study of the area in question that is otherwise characteristic of the scientific approach. Indeed, the exact opposite was true; until recently the subject of death and dying was systematically neglected and avoided by medicine and psychiatry. The possibility of consciousness after death was rejected not because it contradicted clinical observations, but *a priori* because the concept was incompatible with existing scientific theories. However the paradigms in science should not be confused with reality or truth; at best they represent working models that organize existing observations. When they cannot account for and accommodate scientific data of major significance, they have to be replaced by more adequate conceptual frameworks.

The first serious study of near-death experiences was conducted, not by a twentieth-century psychologist or psychiatrist, but by a prominent nineteenth-century Swiss geologist, Albert Heim. After a near-fatal fall in the Alps during which he had a mystical experience, Heim became interested in the subjective experiences associated with life-threatening situations and with dying. Over a period of several decades he collected observations and accounts from numerous survivors of serious accidents: soldiers wounded in battles, masons and roofers who had fallen from heights, workers who survived disasters in mountain projects and railway accidents, and fishermen who had nearly drowned. However, the most important part of Heim's study was based on the accounts of Alpine climbers who had survived near-fatal falls.

Heim first presented his findings in a paper read to a meeting of the Swiss Alpine Club in 1892. His conclusion was that subjective experiences of near-death were strikingly similar in ninety-five per cent of his cases regardless of the surrounding circumstances. Mental activity first became enhanced and accelerated. Perception of events and anticipation of the outcome were unusually clear. Time became greatly expanded, and individuals acted with lightning speed and accurate reality-testing. Typically, this phase was followed by a sudden life-review. The culminating experience was one of transcendental peace, with visions of supernatural beauty and the sound of celestial music.

According to Heim, accidents involving sudden confrontation with death are much more 'horrible and cruel' for the observers than for the victims. In many instances, spectators have been deeply shattered and incapacitated by paralyzing horror and have suffered a lasting trauma, while the victim, if not badly physically injured, comes out of the event free of anxiety and pain.

In 1961 Karlis Osis and his co-workers analyzed more than six hundred questionnaires returned by physicians and nurses detailing the experiences of dying patients. Among the ten per cent of patients who were conscious in the hour before death, a large proportion experienced vivid visions. Some of the images were more or less in accordance with traditional religious concepts, and represented heaven, paradise, or the Eternal City; others were secular images of indescribable beauty, such as exquisite landscapes with exotic birds, or idyllic gardens. Less common were horrifying visions of devils and hell, or frightening sensations such as that of being buried alive. Osis pointed out the similarity of these terminal experiences to the images of eschatological mythology, and also to the psychedelic phenomena induced by LSD or mescaline.

In 1971, Russell Noyes, Professor of Psychiatry at the University of Iowa, studied a large number of subjective accounts of individuals facing death, including Heim's material on Swiss mountain climbers, descriptions of dying in literature and autobiographical accounts by exceptional individuals such as Carl Gustav Jung. Noyes was able to recognize recurrent patterns in these experiences, and to identify three successive stages. The first stage, which he termed *resistance*, was characterized by recognition of danger, fear of death, struggle to save one's life, and finally, acceptance of death. Next followed *life-review*, during which the individual relived important memories or experienced a condensed, panoramic replay of his entire life-trajectory. During the final stage, *transcendence*, the experience was one of mystical, religious, or 'cosmic' states of consciousness.

Noyes' analysis of the death experience is illustrated by the following account of a young woman describing an automobile accident and the inner states that came with it. Her car lost its brakes on a large highway; for several seconds, it skidded uncontrollably on wet pavement, hitting several other cars and finally ending up in the side of a large truck.

> During the several seconds that my car was in motion, I had an experience that seemed to span centuries. I rapidly moved from sheer terror and overwhelming fear for my life to a profound knowledge that I would die. Ironically, with that knowledge came the deepest sense of peace and serenity that I have ever encountered. It was as though I had moved from the periphery of my being – the body that contained me – to the very centre of myself, a place that was imperturbable, totally quiet and at rest. The mantra that I had previously been using in meditation sprang into my consciousness and revolved automatically, with an ease I had never before known. Time seemed to have disappeared as I watched sequences from my life passing before me like a movie, quite rapidly, but with amazing detail. When I reached the point of death, it seemed that I was facing an opaque curtain of some kind. The momentum of the experience carried me, still completely calm, through the curtain and I realized that it had not been a point of termination, but rather of transition. The only way that I can describe the next sensation is to say that every part of me, whatever I was at that moment, felt without

A young woman's portrayal of her confrontation with death. The left of the picture shows her life up to the point of her accident: restricted, bound by time and space, but colourful in patches. At the centre, she reaches a curtain of death, and, passing through it, experiences unity with everything around her. (Collection the authors.)

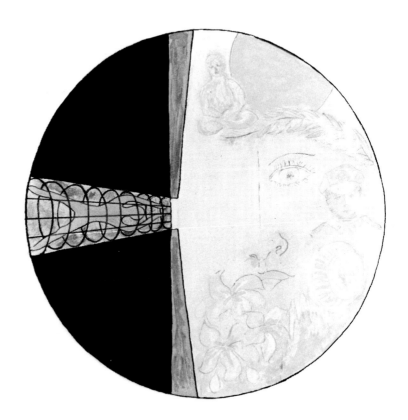

question a far-reaching and encompassing continuum beyond what I had previously thought of as death. It was as though the force that had moved me toward death and then past it would endlessly continue to carry me, through ever-expanding vistas.

It was at this point that my car hit a truck with a great impact. As it came to rest, I looked around and realized that by some miracle I was still alive. And then, an amazing thing happened. As I sat in the midst of the tangled metal, I felt my individual boundaries begin to melt. I started to merge with everything around me – with the policemen, the wreck, the workers with crowbars trying to liberate me, the ambulance, the flowers on a nearby hedge, and the television cameramen. Somewhere, I could see and feel my injuries, but they did not seem to have anything to do with me; they were merely part of a rapidly expanding network that included much more than my body. The sunlight was unusually bright and golden and the entire world seemed to shimmer with a beautiful radiance. I felt blissful and exuberant, even in the middle of the drama around me, and I remained in that state for several days in the hospital. The accident and the experience that accompanied it totally transformed my world-view and my way of understanding existence. Previously, I had not had much interest in spiritual areas and my concept of life was that it was contained between birth and death. The thought of death had always frightened me. I had believed that 'we walk across life's stage but once', and then – nothing. Consequently I had been driven by the fear that I would not have a chance to do all that I wanted to accomplish during my life. Now, the world and my place in it feel completely different. I feel that my self-definition transcends the notion of a limited physical body existing in a limited time frame. I know myself to be part of a larger, unrestricted, creative network that could be described as divine.

Modern Western interest in the subjective experience of dying has been greatly increased by Raymond A. Moody's book *Life After Life*, published in 1975. The author, a physician and psychologist, analyzed 150 accounts of near-death experiences and personally interviewed some fifty people who had survived clinical death. On the basis of his study he was able to isolate certain characteristic elements of the death-experience that occur with great constancy.

A common feature of all the reports was the subject's complaint of the ineffability of these subjective events and the inadequacy of our language to convey their nature. This is a characteristic that death-experiences share with mystical states. Another important element was a convincing sensation of leaving the body. Many people described how, in a comatose state or after physical death, they observed themselves and the scene from above, or from a distance, and heard doctors, nurses and relatives discuss their condition. They were able to witness in detail the various activities carried out by people attending their bodies. Sometimes the accuracy of this perception could be confirmed by subsequent investigation. Out-of-the-body experiences can take a variety of forms. Some people described themselves as amorphous clouds, energy-patterns, or pure consciousness. Others experienced distinct feelings of having a body, but one that was permeable, invisible and inaudible to those in the phenomenal world. Sometimes there was fear, confusion, and a desire to return to the physical body. In other instances people experienced ecstatic feelings of timelessness, weightlessness, serenity and tranquillity. Many people reported hearing peculiar sounds; some of these were distinctly unpleasant noises, others were soothing, such as majestic or transcendental music. There were many descriptions of passing through a dark enclosed place, referred to as a tunnel, cave, funnel, cylinder, valley, trough or sewer. Many people reported encounters with other beings, such as dead relatives or friends, 'guardian spirits' or spirit guides. Particularly common were visions of a 'Being of Light' who appeared as a source of unearthly radiance, yet who showed personal qualities such as love, warmth, compassion and a sense of humour. Communication with this being occurred without words, through an unimpeded transfer of thought. The encounter with the Being of Light was often accompanied by an experience of life-review, and divine judgment or self-judgment.

Moody attempted to reconstruct on the basis of his findings a typical experience of the afterdeath state. Although it is a composite model of this state, based on a large number of accounts rather than an actual individual experience, it is of great interest for our discussion.

A man is dying and, as he reaches the point of greatest physical distress, he hears himself pronounced dead by his doctor. He begins to hear an uncomfortable noise, a loud ringing or buzzing, and at the same time feels himself moving very rapidly through a long dark tunnel. After this, he suddenly finds himself outside of his own physical body, but still in the immediate physical environment, and he sees his own body from a distance, as though he is a spectator. He watches the resuscitation attempt from this unusual vantage point and is in a state of emotional upheaval.

After a while he collects himself and becomes more accustomed to his odd condition. He notices that he still has a 'body', but one of a very different nature and with very different powers from the physical body he has left behind. Soon other things begin to happen. Others come to meet and to help him. He glimpses the spirits of relatives and friends who have already died, and a loving, warm spirit of a kind he has never encountered before – a being of light – appears before him. This being asks him a question, nonverbally, to make him evaluate his life and helps him along by showing him a panoramic, instantaneous playback of the major events of his life. At some point he finds himself approaching some sort of barrier or border, apparently representing the limit between earthly life and the next life. Yet, he finds that he must go back to the earth, that time for his death has not yet come. At this point he resists, for by now he is taken up with his experiences in the afterlife and does not want to return. He is overwhelmed by intense feelings of joy, love, and peace. Despite his attitude, though, he somehow reunites with his physical body and lives.

Later he tries to tell others, but he has trouble doing so. In the first place, he can find no human words adequate to describe these unearthly episodes. He also finds that others scoff, so he stops telling other people. Still the experience affects his life profoundly, especially his views about death and its relationship to life.

There are striking parallels between Moody's observations and descriptions from eschatological literature, particularly the Bardo states in the Tibetan *Book of the Dead*. Similar if not identical elements occur in psychedelic sessions when the subjects experience deep confrontation with death in the context of the death-rebirth process. As we shall see in a later section, there are also correspondences with spontaneously occurring states experienced by some schizophrenic patients.

Images of the Beyond

Comparative studies of concepts of the afterlife have revealed far-reaching similarities among different ethnic and religious groups, even those which had no demonstrable contact before the formation of their eschatological beliefs. The recurrence of certain themes is quite remarkable, particularly for the two polar images of life after death – the abode of the righteous, heaven or paradise, and the place for the wicked, or hell.

The basic experiential characteristics of heaven and hell are always the same – endless joy and bliss for heaven and tortures without end for hell – even though their forms range from concrete representations, resembling terrestrial existence in all important respects, to highly abstract metaphysical formulations. It is not always clear whether those images that are sufficiently concrete for pictorial representation were believed to be literal and accurate descriptions of the afterlife experiences, or metaphors for states of mind that cannot be captured directly by any artistic means.

Modern consciousness-research offers interesting new insight into this problem. In psychedelic sessions, in spontaneous visionary states, and in the

Sisyphus condemned eternally to roll a rock uphill, as punishment for binding Thanatos, i.e., for tricking death. On the left Hera holds ears of corn, on the right is seated Hades, lord of the underworld (After a Greek vase, Staatliche Antikensammlungen, Munich.)

The Greek Ixion suffers endless tortures, bound to a revolving wheel – his punishment by Zeus for attempting the chastity of Hera. (Ixion, after a Greek vase. Berlin Museum.)

practice of experiential psychotherapy, one encounters ecstatic and hellish experiences of an entirely abstract nature as well as concrete and specific images of heavens and hells. It is fascinating to find that occasionally the eschatological symbolism appears to be from a cultural framework entirely unknown to the subject, or totally alien to his background; this observation supports Carl Gustav Jung's concept of the collective and racial unconscious.

Accounts by people who have survived clinical death or near-fatal accidents similarly cover a wide range, varying from descriptions of abstract states to detailed pictorial visions. In describing his early findings, Raymond Moody emphasized the lack of mythological elements such as 'the cartoonist's heaven of pearly gates, golden streets, and winged, harp-playing angels, or a hell of flames and demons with pitchforks'. However, in a recent sequel to his first book, he has reported that he is now finding an increasing number of individuals who during their encounters with death experience concrete and detailed archetypal images of celestial landscapes, with cities of light, radiant palatial mansions, exotic gardens and magnificent rivers. On the negative side, he described experiences of astral realms with perplexed spirits, confused discarnate entities who had not been able to detach themselves fully from the physical world. The problem of figurative versus abstract concepts of the afterlife thus seems to be less a matter of opinion or interpretation, than a reflection of different types or modes of direct experience of the Beyond.

Whether experienced as concrete or abstract, heaven and hell constitute distinct polarities and are in a sense negative images or complementary aspects of each other. In artistic representations of these two abodes of the dead, their antithetical nature is expressed both in the general atmosphere and in every specific detail. Celestial realms are characterized by spaciousness, a sense of freedom and abundance of light. Infernal regions are claustrophobic, nightmarish, oppressive and dark. The same polarity exists in landscape, architecture, typical inhabitants and the experiences of the deceased consigned to these places.

The scenery of the heavens and paradises is typically flooded with brilliant white or golden light, and is full of luminescent clouds or rainbows. Nature is represented by the best it has to offer: fertile soil, fields of ripening grain, beautiful oases or parks, luscious gardens or flourishing meadows. The trees are laden with gorgeous blossoms and bear succulent fruits. The roads are paved with gold, diamond, rubies, emeralds and other precious stones. The paradisiacal landscapes are irrigated by fountains of youth, streams with water of life, clear lakes and rivers of milk, honey and fragrant oil. The celestial architecture is translucent and abounds in palaces glimmering with gold and precious stones. Halls are illumined by sparkling crystal chandeliers and decorated with dancing fountains. The atmosphere is fragrant, permeated with sweet perfumes and exquisite scent of burning incense. In contrast, the infernal scenery is represented as black, barren and desolate. Its fires emit blinding and smothering smoke. The landscapes of hell are dominated by volcanic craters, yawning chasms, jagged cliffs, dark valleys and fuming pits. The paradisiacal trees of life and rich orchards have as their counterparts the infernal spike-trees that are covered with thorns, daggers and swords, and bear poisonous fruit in the shape of demon-heads. Instead of the clear streams and fountains of youth of the garden of love, hell offers dark and dangerous rivers, lakes of fire, stinking pools and treacherous, putrid swamps. The dismal counterparts of the palaces of heaven are sinister and gloomy subterranean mansions surrounded by impassable walls, with inhospitable cold corridors and air contaminated by unimaginable stench. Fiery workshops with high smoke-stacks and glowing furnaces spread sulphuric fumes over the infernal cities.

The same polarity extends to the inhabitants of heaven and hell. The divine beings manifest exquisite beauty; they are ethereal, translucent, radiant and surrounded by auras, haloes or fields of light. In relation to others, they are benevolent, healing, nourishing and protective. The devils or demons are dark and heavy, with bestial characteristics and terrifying appearance. Cruel and malevolent, they represent unbridled instinctual forces. This contrast is most obvious in the case of the supreme rulers of the Beyond, and is best illustrated by the Christian imagery of the triple-headed Satan parodying the Holy Trinity.

Images of the paradises and heavens abound in peacocks, parrots and other exotic birds with brilliant plumage, beautiful butterflies and gentle animals. The infernal menagerie includes eagles, vultures, screech-owls and other vicious predator-birds, bloodthirsty jaguars, hounds, wolves, vampire bats, giant reptiles, poisonous vipers and composite monsters devouring human souls.

In the experience of the souls, the joy, bliss and serenity of the paradisiacal states have as counterparts the bestial tortures of hell and an entire spectrum of emotional agonies. Instead of sweet, harmonious music and songs of praise to the supreme deity, hell resounds with a cacophony of screams, gnashing of teeth, inhuman wailings and pleas for mercy. In contrast to the fragrance of exquisite perfumes and divine incense, the infernos are permeated by the caustic odour of sulphur and the stench of burning rubbish, rotting corpses, dung and offal. The blessed in the celestial realms feast on ambrosia, nectar, Soma and luscious fruits, or are nourished directly by emanations of divine energy. The souls condemned to hell are tormented by hunger and insatiable thirst, and subjected to painful forced ingestion of excrement, or even bits of their own flesh.

In the light of recent observations from consciousness-research, modern science has had to correct its view of heaven and hell. It is now understood that these are experiential states available under certain circumstances to all human beings. As Aldous Huxley pointed out in *Heaven and Hell*, the bliss of the celestial realms and the horrors of hell are rather frequent experiences for psychedelic subjects. These states are also experienced spontaneously during the spiritual emergencies that we call 'acute psychotic episodes'. And we have learned that experiences of heaven and hell are of quite regular occurrence when one is facing biological death. The latter fact suggests that we should re-evaluate our attitude toward eschatological mythology. Instead of representing bizarre and ultimately useless pieces of knowledge, the data about the hells and heavens can prove to be invaluable cartographies of strange experiential worlds which each of us will have to enter at some point in the future.

Christ rescuing the soul from the Devil. (From ms., Speculum Humanae Salvationis, *German, 15th century. John Rylands University Library, Manchester.)*

The posthumous journey of the soul

The images of the abodes of the blessed and the damned represent only one important aspect of the Beyond. In most cultures there is also the concept of the posthumous journey of the soul. The deceased are not transported directly to their final destinations; first they have to undergo a series of unusual adventures, ordeals, and trials. Sometimes these adventures involve travelling through dangerous landscapes not dissimilar to earthly deserts, high mountains, jungles or swamps. The soul may have to encounter and combat various strange beings and fantastic creatures. At other times, the scenery of the Beyond bears very little similarity to anything known on earth. The stages of the posthumous journey may also be represented as sequences of unusual, more or less abstract states of mind instead of concrete places and encounters. A particularly common theme of the afterlife adventures of the soul is that of Divine Judgment. This occurs in various forms not only in the Judaic, Christian, Moslem, Egyptian and Zoroastrian traditions, but also in the Oriental countries such as India, China, Japan and Tibet, and even in the Mesoamerican religions.

If some descriptions of the soul's journey appear simple and naive, others offer complex and sophisticated maps of unusual states of consciousness. In Hinduism, Buddhism and Jainism, the journey is integrated into elaborate cosmological and ontological schemes involving cycles of rebirth, series of individual reincarnations, and the law of karma – the debit and credit balance which is carried over to successive lifetimes.

Two cultures in the history of humanity have shown particularly strong interest in death and dying: the ancient Egyptians and the Tibetans. The priests of these two cultures shared a deep belief in the continuation of consciousness after physical death. They developed elaborate rituals to ease the transition of the deceased to the Beyond, and designed complex cartographies as guides for the journey of the soul. The written forms of these teachings are known in the West as the Egyptian and Tibetan 'Books of the Dead'. These are documents of such relevance that they deserve discussion in this context.

The Egyptian *Book of the Dead* refers to a collection of prayers, incantations, magic spells and mythological stories related to death and afterlife. These funerary texts were known in Egypt as *Pert em hru*, which is usually translated as 'Manifestation in Light' or 'Coming Forth in the Day.' The material of the texts is heterogeneous, and reflects the historical conflict between two powerful religious traditions – the priests of the sun god Amen-Ra and the followers of Osiris. On one hand, the texts put great emphasis on the role of the sun god and his divine retinue. Knowledge of the sacred formulae they offer was expected to provide magical means for the deceased to join the crew of the solar barge and enjoy for eternity blessed life in the presence of the sun god, accompanying him during his journey. On the other hand, the texts reflect the tradition of the ancient mortuary god Osiris, who according to legend was killed by his brother, Set, and resurrected by his two sisters, Isis and Nephthys. After having been brought back to life he became the ruler of the otherworld. In this tradition, the dead were ritually identified with Osiris and could be raised to life again.

The sun god, Amen-Ra, was involved in a complicated series of adventures during his diurnal-nocturnal journey. During the day he crossed the sky in the solar barge; the region through which he passed during the hours of night was the otherworld, or Tuat.

The ancient Egyptians believed that the earth was flat and that the whole of the habitable world – that is, Egypt – was surrounded by a chain of lofty and impassable mountains. The sun rose in the morning from an opening in the eastern part of this mountain range, and in the evening disappeared into another hole in the west. Outside this chain of mountains was the region of the Tuat; it ran parallel with the mountains and was on the plane either of the land or of the sky above it. Beyond the Tuat was another chain of mountains, so that the otherworld was situated in a valley. It was thus separated from Egypt as well as from the luminaries – the sun, moon and stars – that lighted the skies. It was a region of eternal gloom and darkness, and a place of fear and horror.

The Tuat was divided into twelve regions, one for each hour of the night. Each region had a gate protected by three guardian deities, and presented specific dangers for the members of the solar crew. They had to pass through places of blazing fire where heat and vapours destroyed nostrils and mouths. Terrifying beings and fantastic creatures threatened them on their way and had to be overcome. The arch-enemy of the sun god was the giant serpent, Aapep, incarnation of Osiris' brother, Set, who made repeated attempts to devour the solar disc.

A district of the Tuat called Sekhet Aaru, or Fields of Reed, was the kingdom of Osiris. To be admitted to this realm, the dead had to undergo the judgment in the Hall of the Two Truths, or Hall of Maat. In the scale-pans of the Great Balance the heart of the deceased was weighed against a feather symbolizing the Goddess of Justice, Maat. The scale was attended by the jackal-headed god, Anubis, while the ibis-headed scribe of the gods, Thoth, recorded the verdict. The composite monster Amemet, Devourer of Souls, combining crocodile, lion and hippopotamus, stood ready to swallow those who failed to pass the judgment.

Traversing the dark valley of the otherworld was perilous for both humans and gods. The only certain safe passage through the Tuat was that of the sun god, since his triumph and rebirth were manifest every morning with the sun's rising in the east. For the followers of the sun god, the goal in the afterlife was to join the solar crew and accompany the sun god during his journey for all eternity. For the followers of Osiris, the sun barge was to carry them to Sekhet Aaru, the kingdom of the god-king Osiris, where they would disembark and attempt to pass the judgment, so that they could stay forever in Osiris' kingdom.

Like the ancient Egyptian culture, the Tibetan was entirely oriented towards the spiritual, and, until quite recently, preserved a wealth of knowledge about the deeper questions of inner life and meaning. For any culture which is primarily concerned with meaning, the study of death – the only certainty that life holds for us – must be central, for an understanding of death is the key to liberation in life.

In the Tibetan tradition, dying, no less than living, is to be performed in complete awareness. For the enlightened, the time, place and circumstances of death are no longer fortuitous. Dying is undertaken consciously. The spirit is transferred, and the body is transformed into the elements, so that no traces of it remain. This phenomenal feat, known as the 'Great Transfer', is exceedingly rare; more common, but still extremely rare (although documented as recently as the 1950s in China), is what is known as the 'Rainbow Body'. Here, seven days after death, only the nails and hair – i.e. the impurities – of the dead person remain. If liberation is not achieved during life, then the opportunities to attain it need to be recognized shortly after death, and for this purpose, the *Book of the Dead* is studied.

The Tibetan *Book of the Dead*, or *Bardo Thödol*, is of more recent origin than its Egyptian counterpart. Although it was clearly based on a much older secret oral tradition, it was first put into its written form in the eighth century AD by Padma Sambhava who introduced Buddhism to Tibet. The *Bardo Thödol* is a guide through the 'Bardos' or intermediate states between death and rebirth. The information it provides is quite specific, even as to the duration of the stay in various realms, or states of consciousness. Its purpose is to allow the deceased to recognize as opportunities for liberation the states with which he has already become acquainted during his practice. This recognition is likened to that which a son has for his mother. After death, the understanding achieved through instruction and practice during life, known as the 'Son Wisdom', recognizes the 'Mother Wisdom' of light and true clarity.

The first part of the *Bardo Thödol*, called *Chikhai Bardo*, describes the experience of dissolution at the moment of death, when the departed have a blinding vision of the Primary Clear Light of Pure Reality. At this instant they may attain liberation if they can recognize the light and are not deterred by its overwhelming intensity. Those whose lack of preparation causes them to lose this opportunity will have another chance later on, when the Secondary Clear Light dawns upon them. If they do not succeed this time either, they will undergo a complicated sequence of experiences during the following Bardos, when their consciousness becomes progressively estranged from the liberating truth, as they approach another rebirth.

In the *Chönyid Bardo*, or the 'Bardo of the Experiencing of Reality', the departed are confronted with a succession of deities: the Peaceful Deities enveloped in brilliant-coloured lights, the Wrathful Deities, the Doorkeeping Deities, the Knowledge-Holding Deities, and the Yoginis of the Four Cardinal Points. Simultaneously with the powerful vision of these deities, the departed perceive dull lights of various colours, indicating the individual *lokas*, or realms into which they can be born: the realm of the gods (*devaloka*), the realm of the titans (*asuraloka*), the realm of the humans (*manakaloka*), the realm of brute subhuman creatures (*tiryakaloka*), the realm of the hungry ghosts (*pretaloka*), and the realm of hell (*narakaloka*). Attraction to these lights will thwart spiritual liberation and facilitate rebirth.

If the departed miss the opportunities for liberation offered in the first two Bardos, they will enter the *Sidpa Bardo*, or the 'Bardo of Seeking Rebirth'. At this stage they experience their Bardo bodies, which are not composed of gross matter, but are endowed with the power of unimpeded motion and the ability to pass through solid objects. The karmic record of the deceased – the sum of moral debits or credits – determines whether they will experience happiness or misery in this Bardo. Those who have accumulated much bad karma will be tortured by confrontations with beasts of prey or the raging forces of nature. Those whose karmic merits are paramount will experience delightful pleasures, while those with neutral karma will find at this stage only a colourless stupidity and indifference.

An important element of this Bardo is the judgment in which Dharma Raja, King and Judge of the Dead, examines the past deeds of the deceased with the mirror of karma. This mirror reveals all good and evil deeds, which are weighed against each other in the form of white and black pebbles. From the court, six karmic pathways lead to the various realms to which the dead are assigned according to their merits or demerits. During the *Sidpa Bardo* it is essential for the departed to realize that all these beings and events are the projections of their own minds, and are essentially void. If this opportunity is missed, rebirth will inevitably follow. All that the *Bardo Thödol* can offer at this point is techniques of closing the doors of undesirable wombs and help in choosing the least unfavourable rebirth.

Although the Egyptian and the Tibetan *Books of the Dead* are certainly the best known examples of their kind, they are by no means unique. Similar literature exists in other traditions; the Moslem, Hindu, Chinese and Japanese Buddhist and Mesoamerican eschatological texts can be cited as examples. It is generally less well known that the ancient *Books of the Dead* have their counterpart in our own cultural tradition. Toward the end of the Middle Ages, the works usually globally referred to as *Ars Moriendi* or *The Art of Dying* were widespread in many European countries, particularly in Austria, Germany, France and Italy. The literature of this kind falls into two categories: the first consisting of books focusing on the experience of dying and on the art of guiding the dying on their last journey; the second, of texts that deal with the relevance of death for life.

Texts in the first category are a rich repository of knowledge about important experiential aspects of dying. This can be illustrated by the phenomenon described as attacks of Satan, interpreted by Church authorities as attempts by evil forces to divert souls from their way to Heaven by powerful interventions at the most strategic and crucial time. Most of the manuals discuss five major attacks of the Devil: serious doubts regarding faith; desperation and agonizing qualms of conscience; impatience and irritability due to suffering; conceit, vanity and pride; greed, avarice and other worldly concerns and attachments. These attempts of the Devil are counteracted by divine influences that give the dying a foretaste of Heaven, a sense of being subjected to supreme judgment, a feeling of obtaining higher help, and a promise of redemption. Modern consciousness-research has demonstrated that many of these experiences actually do occur when people are facing death symbolically in psychedelic sessions, or suffering severe biological crises. There is no doubt that the descriptions of dying in the *Ars Moriendi* literature and other similar manuals should be taken seriously; they represent surprisingly accurate experiential maps, rather than arbitrary imaginary constructs.

The texts related to the process of biological death also offer concrete instructions for the dying and their helpers, to guide them during the last hours. Most medieval death-manuals agree that it is essential to create the right disposition and right attitude in the dying. It is absolutely mandatory not to instil false hopes of recovery. All possible support should be given to the dying to help them face death and accept it. Courageous confrontation of death is seen as crucial; avoidance and reluctance to surrender are considered two of the major dangers the dying person faces. Some of the manuals explicitly state that it is less objectionable and harmful for the helpers to evoke fears in the dying that later prove unfounded than for them to allow the individual to use denial and die unprepared.

The second category of texts in the *Ars Moriendi* literature emphasizes the importance of awareness and understanding of death for right living; its powerful imagery stresses the impermanence of existence, the omni-presence of death, and the meaninglessness of all wordly pursuits. In the recent past, this preoccupation with impermanence, expressed in contemplation of death and contempt of the world, was seen by Western scientists as a symptom of social pathology. Yet according to the observations from LSD research and experiential psychotherapies, deep confrontation with the most frightening and repulsive aspects of human existence can result in a spiritual opening, and a qualitatively different way of being in the world.

The dual orientation of the *Ars Moriendi* – towards death and life – seems to be characteristic of all 'books of the dead'. The message they communicate teaches us not only about death, but about an alternative approach to life mediated by the experience of death. This issue is of such fundamental significance that we will discuss it in more detail.

Ritual encounters with death

The opportunity to experience death without actually dying, visit the realm of the dead and return, or communicate with the world of spirits, has been offered in many different frameworks since the dawn of human history. The most ancient example of this kind of experience is to be found in the phenomenon of shamanism. The core of the initiation trials of the Siberian and Ural-Altaic shamans is a profound encounter with death in the form of ritual annihilation and rebirth. Many shamans have reported that during their 'initiatory illness' they lay in their tents or in some solitary place in a condition near to death for between three and seven days. During this time they experienced a journey into the underworld where they were attacked by demons and ancestral spirits, and exposed to a variety of extreme tortures. Although there is considerable variation in the details of these ordeals among individual shamans and also among different tribes, all share the general atmosphere of horror, torture and inhuman suffering. The ordeals involve dismemberment, disposal of body fluids, scraping of the flesh from the bones and tearing of the eyes from the sockets. After the novice shaman has been reduced to a skeleton, the pieces of the body are shared among the spirits of different diseases. Then the aspirant receives new flesh and blood, and experiences a magical flight or ascent to the heavenly regions on a rainbow, a birch-tree or a pole. During this process of

According to medieval belief, at the time of death the diabolic forces make their last desperate attempt to divert the soul from its way to Heaven. The 'assaults of Satan' illustrated are the temptation through vanity, the temptation through avarice, and the temptation through impatience. (Ars Moriendi, c. 1465, British Library London.)

Persephone with her husband Pluto in the underworld where she was condemned to pass a third of each year. (Persephone and Pluto, from a Greek cup, 5th century BC. British Museum, London.)

death and rebirth, supernatural knowledge or power is received from semi-divine beings with human or animal forms. Initiatory death is always followed by resurrection, and resolution of the shaman's crisis. Shamans are equally at home in 'objective reality' and the various regions of the supernatural world. They become healers, seers and priests, and accompany the souls of the dead during their journey to the otherworld.

Many mythologies are concerned with the theme of death and rebirth. Heroes descend into the underworld and after enduring extreme ordeals and overcoming obstacles, return to earth endowed with supernatural powers. Gods, demigods, or heroes die or are killed and are brought back to life in a new role, rejuvenated and immortal. In a less obvious symbolic form, the same theme is sometimes expressed by the image of a hero devoured and regurgitated by a terrifying monster.

In many places of the world and in different historical periods, mythological figures and stories of this kind became the central focus of sacred mysteries in which neophytes experienced ritual death and rebirth. The Babylonian-Assyrian rites of Tammuz and Ishtar, originating probably before 4000 BC, provide one of the earliest examples of the allegory of the dying god. It is the story of the mother goddess, Ishtar, who descends into the underworld in search of the sacred elixir that will revive her dead son and husband, Tammuz. In the ancient Egyptian mysteries of Isis and Osiris, the mythological model for ritual transformation was the murder and dismemberment of Osiris by his brother Set, and his magical resurrection by his sisters, Isis and Nephthys. Mysteries of this kind were particularly abundant in ancient Greece and the neighbouring countries. The famous Eleusinian mysteries in Attica were based on an esoteric interpretation of the myth about the fertility goddess Demeter and her daughter Persephone, kidnapped by the chthonic god Pluto. This myth, usually seen as a symbolic allegory of seasonal cycles and growth of vegetation, became for initiates a metaphor for spiritual transformation. The Orphic cult, Dionysian rites, and the mysteries of Attis and Adonis, though based on different mythological stories, all had the same core – the theme of death and rebirth. Similar rituals were practised among the Norsemen, in the Mithraic religion, in the Hermetic tradition, in India and Tibet, among various African tribes, in Pre-Columbian societies, and in many other cultures of the world.

Discussion of the confrontation with death in a ritual context would be incomplete without mention of rites of passage, in which the initiates are not a chosen few, but entire social groups or even cultures. Rites of passage are powerful transformative rituals, usually enacted at the time of biological transitions such as birth, circumcision, puberty, marriage, second maturity and death. Van Gennep, who first defined and described these rites, noticed that they have three characteristic phases. In the first phase, which he called *separation*, the initiates are removed from their social matrix and kept in isolation for weeks or even months. During this time, they are learning through songs, dances, tales and myths about the strange experiential territory they are about to enter. In the second phase, *transition*, powerful mind-altering techniques are used to provide a transforming experience. These methods include combinations of sleep-deprivation, fasting, pain,

mutilation, group pressure, social isolation, emotional and physical stress, and in some instances the use of psychedelic substances. The initiates experience extremes of anguish, chaos, confusion and liminality, and emerge from the process of annihilation with a sense of rejuvenation and rebirth. The third stage, *incorporation*, involves the reintegration of the transformed individual into the community in a new role. The depth and intensity of the death-rebirth experience provides a dramatic framework for the termination of the old social role and the assumption of the new one. However, repeated encounters with annihilation followed by a sense of redefinition have another important function: they prepare the individual for eventual biological death by establishing a deep, almost cellular awareness that periods of destruction are those of transition rather than termination.

Death and rebirth in schizophrenia and psychedelic states

As we mentioned earlier, psychology and psychiatry have usually treated the concepts of consciousness after death and the posthumous journey of the soul as products of primitive magical thinking, or reaction-formation against the fear of death and impermanence. Until recently, it was rarely seriously considered that the descriptions of the adventures of the soul after death could reflect experiential reality. Similarly, the accounts of shamanic journeys, temple mysteries and rites of passage were viewed in terms of primitive superstition, group suggestion or collective psychopathology. The descriptions of heaven, hell and the posthumous adventures of the soul were misunderstood – frequently not only by critics of religion, but by clergy and theologians themselves – as historical and geographical references rather than cartographies of unusual states of consciousness. As such, they were not taken seriously because they appeared to be incompatible with the scientific world-view.

However, recent developments in modern consciousness-research have brought some unexpected observations, suggesting that Western science might have been somewhat premature in its judgments of ancient and non-Western systems of thought and spiritual practices.

It has been known for a long time that some schizophrenic patients suffering from acute episodes or chronic psychotic states describe profound experiences of a religious or mystical nature, closely resembling the descriptions found in eschatological literature. Such experiences include a vivid and convincing sense of encounters with demons, inhuman tortures in hell, scenes of Divine Judgment or, conversely, meetings with saints, angels, spirit guides and other celestial beings – even union with God. In some instances, the experiences transcend the traditional Christian framework, and involve phenomena similar to those described in the Oriental literature, such as memories of past incarnations, and the Bardo states of the Tibetan *Book of the Dead*.

Another type of schizophrenic experience which is especially relevant for an understanding of death and dying is that of death-rebirth. Many patients suffering from acute psychotic episodes report dramatic experiences of death and rebirth, or even of the destruction and recreation of the entire world. In the rare instances when such experiences are completed and well integrated, the patients frequently reach a better level of mental functioning and social adjustment than they had before. This process bears a deep similarity to the ritual transformation described in temple mysteries or the rites of passage of preliterate societies.

As a result of clinical work with schizophrenics, psychiatrists have realized that the eschatological descriptions found in the religious scriptures represent experiential realities rather than reflecting anxious denial of death and wishful fantasy. This has inspired a trend among Western scientists to move religious beliefs from the category of primitive superstition to the area of psychopathology.

Important new evidence became available during the fifties and sixties, when experimental psychiatry achieved epoch-making discoveries in the area of psychedelic research. This development was triggered by the discovery in April 1943, by the Swiss chemist Albert Hofmann, of the psychoactive properties of diethylamide of lysergic acid or LSD-25. When this new, powerful, psychedelic substance became available for researchers throughout the world, it was possible to explore systematically and on a larger scale a phenomenon that historians and anthropologists had known for a long time: that certain drugs can produce in otherwise normal individuals deep mystical and religious states, including shattering eschatological visions.

The fact that psychedelics, with their amplifying and catalyzing effect on the human mind, induce experiences of this kind in randomly selected experimental subjects, clearly suggests that matrices for such experiences exist in the unconscious as a normal constituent of the human personality.

Although scientific interest in psychedelic substances is relatively recent, their ritual use can be traced back to the dawn of human history. From time immemorial, plants containing powerful mind-altering substances have been used for the diagnosing and healing of diseases, enhancement of paranormal abilities, and for magical or ritual purposes. Plants buried with a shaman discovered during the excavations of the New Stone Age settlement of Çatal Hüyük in Turkey were identified by pollen analysis as psychedelic. Reports of hallucinogenic drug-use in Chinese medicine span a period of more than 3,500 years. The legendary divine potion of Vedic literature, Soma, was used by the Indoiranian tribes several millennia ago. Various preparations from hemp, *Cannabis indica* and *sativa*, have been known in Asia and Africa for many centuries under different names, and have been used in folk-medicine and religious ceremonies as well as for recreation and pleasure. In the Middle Ages, potions and ointments containing psychoactive plants were widely used in the Witches' Sabbath and Black Mass rituals. The most famous ingredients of witches' brews were the deadly nightshade or *Atropa Belladonna*; thorn-apple or *Datura Stramonium*; mandrake or *Mandragora officinarum*; and henbane or *Hyoscyamus niger*. The use of psychedelic substances has a long history in Central America among the Aztecs, Mayans and Olmecs. The most famous of these plants are the Mexican cactus *Lophophora Williamsii* (peyote), the sacred mushroom *Psilocybe mexicana* (teonanacatl), and several varieties of *Ipomoea*, the source of morning glory seeds (ololiuqui). Among African tribes, preparations from the eboga plant, *Tabernanthe iboga*, are used as a sacrament. South American Indians of the Amazon region prepare a powerful psychedelic potion, *ayahuasca* or *yage*, whose major ingredient is the jungle *liana Banisteriopsis Caapi*. Ritual ingestion of the fly-agaric mushroom *Amanita muscaria* is important in shamanic practices among certain Siberian tribes such as the Koryaks, Samoyeds and Chukchees.

As Aldous Huxley pointed out in his essay *Heaven and Hell*, many subjects experience in psychedelic sessions states of ecstatic rapture and extreme horrors that are indistinguishable from those described in the scriptures of the great religions of the world. The possibility of triggering such religious and mystical experiences under laboratory conditions and subjecting them to direct study offered hope of fascinating insights into the psychology and psychopathology of religion.

The most interesting aspect of psychedelic substances, from this point of view, is the fact that they can induce, without any specific programming and guidance, profound death-rebirth experiences, and facilitate spiritual opening. The human unconscious, activated chemically, actually tends to enact spontaneously a powerful confrontation with death that can result in transcendence.

After LSD subjects have moved beyond the more superficial levels of the psychedelic experience, the sensory barrier and biographically determined content, the sessions focus on the problems of the impermanence of existence, physical pain, emotional agony, aging and decrepitude, and ultimately, dying and death. Sessions of this kind are characterized by preoccupation with death, with visions of people dying, epidemics, scenes of war and devastation, cemeteries and funerals. The most important element of this process, however, is an extremely realistic sense of the ultimate biological crisis, fully comparable with actual dying. It is not uncommon for the subject to lose the insight that the psychedelic session is a symbolic experience, and to develop a delusional conviction that biological death is imminent.

This shattering encounter with the extremes of human existence has two important consequences. The first is a profound existential crisis that forces the individual to question seriously the meaning of human life, and to re-evaluate his own system of basic values. Worldly ambitions, competitive drives, and the craving for power, fame and possessions tend to fade away when viewed against the background of the mandatory ending of each human drama in physical annihilation. The second important consequence is the opening of spiritual areas of the unconscious that are intrinsic parts of the structure of human personality, and are independent of the individual's racial, cultural and religious background. They thus belong to the realm of the collective unconscious (in Carl Gustav Jung's terminology), and can be referred to as archetypal.

Confrontation with death is just one aspect of the psychedelic experience. A second important aspect is the struggle to be reborn, conceptualized by many subjects as the reliving of their birth trauma. In the death-rebirth process, dying, being born and giving birth are intimately interwoven. Sequences of extreme emotional and physical suffering are followed by experiences of liberation, birth or rebirth, with visions of brilliant white or golden light.

The amalgam of dying, being born and giving birth results in a sense of destruction of the old personality-structure and the birth of a new self. This process bears a striking similarity to the events described through the ages in shamanic initiation, rites of passage, temple mysteries, and in the ecstatic religions of many ancient and preliterate cultures.

The rich and complex phenomena of the psychedelic death-rebirth process appear in several patterns that the subjects often relate to the stages of biological birth. In psychedelic therapy, all these patterns must be experienced repeatedly and in different sequences before the process is completed.

The first type of psychedelic experience on this level may be termed *cosmic engulfment*. Subjects often relate this phase to the onset of biological delivery, when the original equilibrium of the intrauterine existence is disturbed, first by chemical signals and later by contractions of the uterus. The experience of cosmic engulfment begins with an overwhelming feeling of anxiety and an awareness of vital threat. The source of danger cannot be clearly identified, and the individual tends to interpret the immediate environment or the whole world in paranoid terms. An intensification of anxiety usually leads to the experience of being sucked into a gigantic whirlpool. A frequent symbolic variant of this phase of engulfment is being swallowed by a terrifying monster – a dragon, whale, tarantula, octopus or crocodile – or of descending into the underworld and encountering its threatening creatures. There is a clear parallel with eschatological visions of the gaping jaws of the gods of death, mouths of Hell, or the descent of heroes into the underworld. The expulsion from the Garden of Eden and the theme of the Fall of Rebel Angels belong to this experiential matrix.

Odin at the entrance to the otherworld. (Drawing by Fuseli, 19th century. British Museum, London.)

The second constellation, the experience of *no exit*, is related by subjects to the first clinical stage of birth when uterine contractions encroach on the foetus but the cervix is still closed. The world appears dark and menacing; the subject apprehends the situation as a claustrophobic nightmare and suffers acute mental and physical tortures. In this context, it is impossible to foresee that the agony can ever end. Human existence appears devoid of meaning, utterly absurd or even monstrous. The chief characteristic that differentiates this pattern from the one following is the unique emphasis on the role of the victim, and the fact that the situation is inescapable and eternal. There is no hope, and there appears to be no way out, either in space or in time. Many psychedelic subjects have indicated independently that this experience appears to be the psychological prototype for the religious concept of hell.

The third pattern on this level is that of the *death-rebirth struggle*. Many of its aspects can be understood if we relate it to the second stage of delivery in which uterine contractions continue but the cervix stands open. It is the time of gradual propulsion through the birth canal, involving mechanical crushing pressures, struggle for survival, and often a high degree of suffocation. In the terminal phases of delivery, the foetus experiences immediate contact with a variety of biological materials, such as blood, mucus, foetal liquid, urine and even faeces. From the experiential point of view, this pattern is rather complex and has several important facets: the atmosphere of a titanic struggle, sadomasochistic sequences, various deviant forms of intense sexual arousal, scatological involvement and the element of purifying fire (pyrocatharsis).

LSD subjects experience in this phase powerful currents of energy streaming through their bodies, and accumulations of enormous tension alternating with explosive discharges. This is typically associated with images of raging elements of nature, apocalyptic war-scenes and displays of aggressive technology. An enormous amount of energy is being discharged and consumed in vivid destructive and self-destructive experiences. At times, sexual arousal can reach an unnaturally high degree and be expressed in visions of orgies, various perverted activities or rhythmic sensual dances. The scatological facet of the death-rebirth struggle involves an intimate encounter with repulsive biological material. Subjects can experience themselves as wallowing in excrement, drowning in cesspools, crawling in rotting offal or tasting blood. There often follows an experience of passing through purifying fire in preparation for spiritual rebirth.

This experiential phase is distinguished from the 'no exit' constellation by the subject's sense that he is not helpless and the situation is not hopeless; suffering has a definite purpose. The accompanying emotions are a mixture of agony and ecstasy. The images that occur in this context represent battles between the forces of good and evil: the drama of Divine Judgment, scenes of the temptation of saints, of Purgatory or martyr-death. The strange mixture of religiosity, death, anxiety, sex, aggression, and scatology typical for this matrix explains the frequent occurrence of images related to blasphemic rituals of the Valpurgi's Night and satanic orgies, or, conversely, to the bestiality of the Inquisition.

The pattern of *death and rebirth* is related to the third clinical stage of delivery. The propulsion through the birth canal is completed, and is followed by explosive relief and relaxation. After the umbilical cord is cut, physical separation from the mother is accomplished and the child starts its new existence as an anatomically independent individual.

The 'death and rebirth' phase represents the termination and resolution of the 'death-rebirth struggle'. Suffering and agony culminate in an experience of total annihilation on all levels – physical, emotional, intellectual, moral and transcendental. This is usually referred to as the 'ego death'; it seems to involve instantaneous destruction of all the individual's previous reference-points. Such annihilation is often followed by visions of

Painting from a psychedelic session depicting the experience of spiritual rebirth. The subject is naked, facing and embracing the sun. (Collection Dr Milan Hausner.)

blinding white or golden light and a sense of liberating decompression and expansion. The universe is perceived as indescribably beautiful and radiant; subjects feel themselves cleansed and purged, and speak of redemption, salvation, *moksha,* or *samadhi.* Numerous images of emerging into light from darkness, glorious opening of heavens, revelation of the divine, slaying of dragons, harrowing of Hell, beating of demons, chaining of the devil, and the final victory of the pure religious impulse, express this state of consciousness. In the corresponding shamanic process, annihilation and dismemberment are followed by ascent to the heavenly realms in a new body. In death-rebirth mythologies, the correspondence is with the revival or resurrection of the sacrificed god.

If the patterns of psychedelic experience so far described may be likened to stages of the birth process, the mystical experience of *cosmic unity* seems to be related to the primal oneness of foetus and mother. When no noxious stimuli interfere, conditions for the foetus are close to ideal, involving total protection and security and continuous satisfaction of all needs. The basic characteristics of this experience are transcendence of the subject-object dichotomy, feelings of sacredness, moving beyond the boundaries of time and space, ineffable bliss, and insights of cosmic relevance. The archetypal visions accompanying the experience of cosmic unity are of heavens, celestial cities, paradisiacal gardens, and radiant divine beings. This state is also typically associated with images of aquatic and oceanic scenes or of galactic vistas. As in the previous examples, these images come from the collective unconscious and are independent of the racial, cultural and educational background of the subject.

Another important category of psychedelic experiences can best be categorized as *transpersonal*. These experiences involve conscious identification with persons, animals or other entities that in the usual state of consciousness would clearly be considered outside the framework of the individual. Some experiences belonging to this category can be interpreted as regression in historical time and exploration of one's own biological or spiritual past. It is not infrequent in psychedelic states to experience quite concrete and realistic episodes that take the form of foetal or embryonal memories. Many subjects have reported vivid sequences experienced on the level of cellular consciousness that seemed to reflect their existence in the form of the sperm or ovum at the moment of conception. Sometimes the regression appears to go even further, and the individual has a convinced feeling of reliving memories from the lives of ancestors, or even of drawing on the racial and collective unconscious. On occasion, LSD subjects have reported experiences in which they identified with various animals on the evolutionary ladder, or had distinct feelings of reliving memories of their existence in a previous incarnation.

Other transpersonal phenomena involve transcendence of spatial rather than temporal barriers. The experience of the consciousness of another person or group of persons, of the population of an entire country, or even of all mankind, are examples. One can also transcend the limits of the specifically human experience and tune in to what appears to be the consciousness of animals, plants or even inanimate objects. At the extreme, it is possible to experience consciousness of all creation, of the whole planet or of the entire material universe. Another phenomenon related to the transcendence of usual spatial limitation is consciousness of certain parts of the body, such as various organs and tissues, or even individual cells.

An important category of transpersonal experiences, involving transcendence of time and space, includes ESP phenomena such as out-of-the-body experience, telepathy, precognition, clairvoyance and clair-audience, space and time travel.

In a large group of transpersonal experiences, the extension of consciousness seems to go beyond the phenomenal world and beyond the space-time continuum as we normally perceive it. Quite common are experiences of encounters with spirits of dead persons or suprahuman spiritual entities. LSD subjects also report numerous visions of archetypal forms, deities and demons – even complex mythological sequences. Intuitive understanding of universal symbols, or the arousal of the inner cosmic energy (Kundalini) and the activation of the centres of the psychic body (chakras), are additional examples in this category. At the extreme, the individual consciousness seems to encompass the totality of existence and identify with the Universal Mind. The ultimate experience appears to be that of the mysterious primordial emptiness and nothingness that contains all of existence in a germinal form, the Void.

Epilogue

During the rapid development of materialistic science, the old beliefs and concepts of exoteric religion were condemned as naive and absurd. It is only now that we can see again that these mythologies and concepts of God, heaven and hell do not refer to physical entities, events in time or geographical locations, but to psychic realities experienced during altered states of consciousness. These realities are an intrinsic part of the human personality that cannot be repressed and denied without serious damage to the quality of human life. For the full expression of human nature, they must be recognized, acknowledged and explored, and in this exploration, the traditional depictions of the afterlife can be our guides.

There now exists extensive clinical evidence to support the claims of religion and mythology that biological death is the beginning of an adventure in consciousness. The 'maps' of the initial stages of this adventure contained in eschatological mythology have proved to be remarkably accurate (though whether the descriptions of the later stages of the afterlife are equally accurate must still remain an open question). However, this perennial wisdom concerning death has another immediate and verifiable dimension – its relevance for life.

Confrontation with death in a ritual context, or precipitated by emotional or spiritual crises, can both eliminate the fear of death and lead to transformation – that is, to a more enlightened and personally satisfying way of living. The spiritual crises of schizophrenia, when they include elements of the death-rebirth process, can, if approached with understanding, become unique moments of growth and restructuring. Similarly, the experiences of death and rebirth induced by psychedelics can sometimes radically alter the patient's attitude to death and dying, alleviate pain and distress, and result in spiritual opening.

The Tibetan tradition emphasizes the vital importance of a lifetime spent in learning and training to distinguish the clear light of truth from the illusory states of unenlightened existence, so that in the confusion immediately following death, this discrimination can still be made. For the Tibetan and many other traditions, the 'way' is to live one's life in the constant awareness of death, and the goal, to die consciously. Such an understanding of the relation of life and death can only throw into sharp relief the negative attitude towards the adventure of death that has recently held the West so firmly in its grip.

Bird of immortality, the peacock
appears in many traditions as a
symbol of Paradise, rebirth and the
incorruptibility of the soul. During
the first ten centuries of Christianity
the peacock was a popular symbol
for Christ. In the East, it represents
rebirth in the imagery of Hinduism,
Buddhism and Islam. (Illumination
by Florentius for the Moralia in Job,
Spain, 945.)

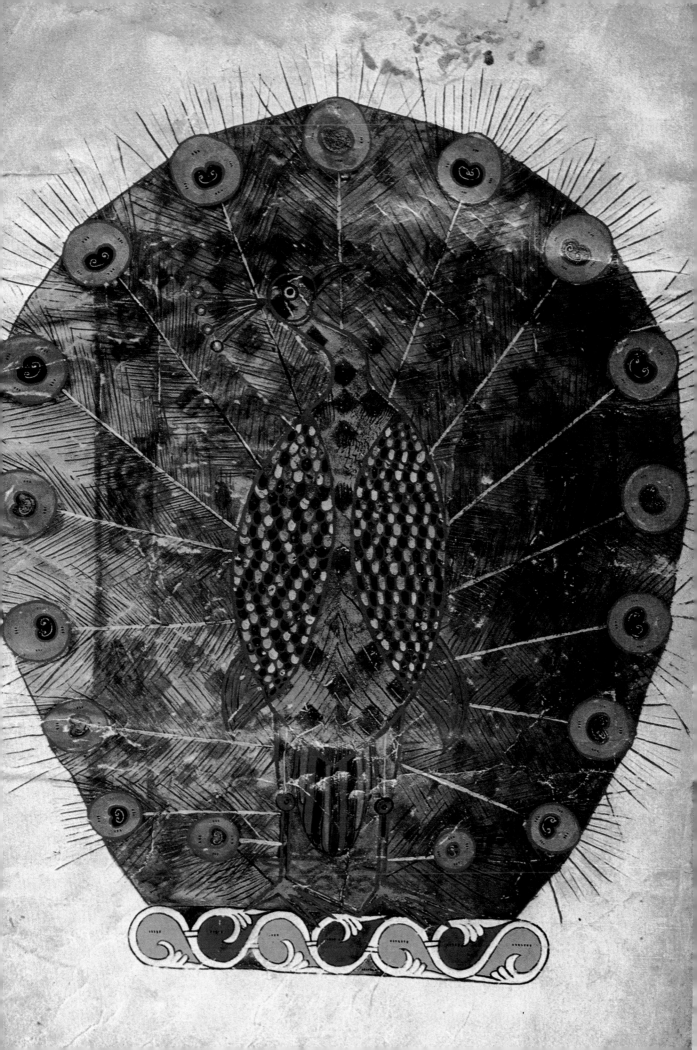

The radiance, benevolence and
beauty of the beings of Paradise
convey the inner tranquillity and
bliss that are to be obtained when
the right relationship of life and

death is understood. In the Buddhist Tusita Paradise, Bodhisattva Maitreya awaits the time when he will come to the world as a Buddha, the 'All-benign', to help all sentient beings to achieve enlightenment. Enveloped in brilliant light, he wears a crown with peacock-feather designs. An Apsara, celestial nymph, holding a sapu-blossom and a lotus, symbol of spiritual rebirth, enlivens Paradise with her graceful presence. (Bodhisattva Maitreya, tanka, Tibet. Apsara, detail of wall-painting from Sigiriya, Ceylon, 5th century AD.)

The experience of 'paradise' is often one of exquisite, abundant, protected nature. The flowering trees of these Paradise scenes are an image for the blossoming self, the harmonious and fruitful centre of the being.

Mohammad on his miraculous Night Journey, riding the mythical mare Burâq, is guided by the Archangel Gabriel through the Moslem paradise garden where dark-eyed houris playfully exchange bouquets. In the Aztec paradise, Tlalocan, the rain god Tlaloc awaits those who have died water-related deaths. The god sits at the base of a magnificent tree with health-giving rain pouring from his hands. On either side, priests make offerings and plant seeds in the fertile earth. Below, the souls in Tlalocan play games, sing songs and chase butterflies. Souls remain for four years in Tlalocan, the most earthly of the three Aztec paradises, before being reborn in another lifetime. (Mohammad's Night Journey, from an illuminated ms., *Mirâj Nâmeh*, East Turkey, 15th century. Tlalocan fresco from Tepantitla, Mexico, 4–8th century.)

The dying and those experiencing symbolic death in psychedelic sessions frequently speak of visions of resplendent palaces and shining celestial cities. Paradise as the Heavenly City represents nature ordered and transformed, the precious stone, a citadel only to be entered with a key – the key of knowledge. In Christian tradition the most famous description of the Heavenly City or New Jerusalem occurs in the Revelation of St John, where it is described as having twelve gates guarded by angels and shining like a precious stone,

illumined by the glory of God. In alchemy, the Heavenly City is referred to as the Great Stone. The biblical vision of the New Jerusalem incorporates all the important elements of the alchemical process called rubedo : the sparkling stone, the heavenly marriage, the conquest of death, the water of life and its fountain, the tree of life and its fruits, and the god of the end and the beginning. Above, a combined paradise garden and Celestial City is unlocked by St Peter, while inside the walls, Abraham, Isaac and Jacob harbour

the homecoming souls in sacred napkins.

The remote paradise of the Hindu god Shiva on Mount Kailasa in Tibet (right) is lively with celestial beings and sages celebrating his sacred marriage to the goddess Parvati. In Tantric tradition, ritual intercourse is a vehicle for transcendence, mirroring the cosmic union of the male and female principles. (St Peter unlocks the Gates of Paradise, wall-painting from Rila Monastery, Bulgaria, 19th century. Shiva and Parvati enthroned, Rajput painting, India, late 18th century.)

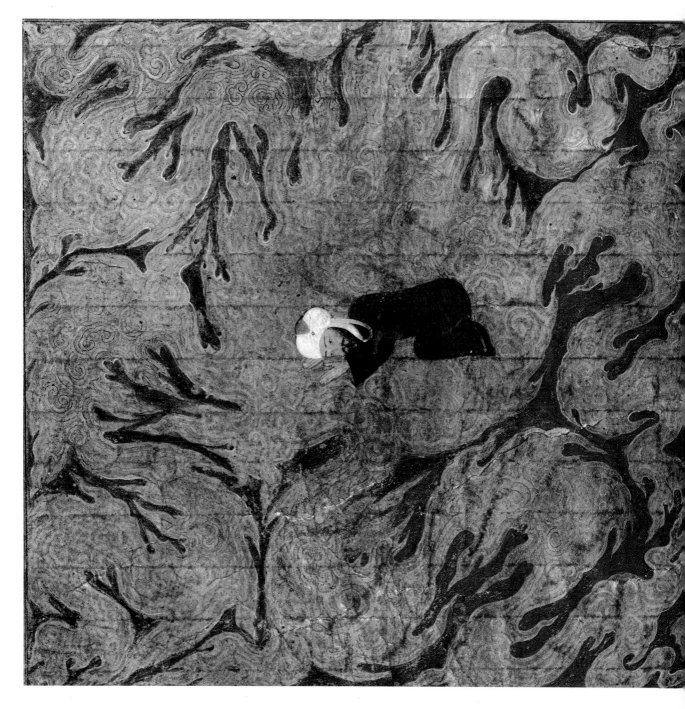

The lustre of gold and precious stones is an approximation in the material world for the ineffable light perceived in mystical experience. In his essay 'Why are Precious Stones Precious?', Aldous Huxley suggests that the excessive value assigned to gold and gems reflects a craving for transcendence.

The palaces of Sukhavati, the Western Paradise of the Mahayana Buddhist Pure Land or Jodo sect, are rich with gold and gems. Entry into this paradise, regarded as a stepping-stone on the path towards enlightenment and Nirvana, is achieved by faith in and surrender to Amitabha, the Lord of Boundless Light.

The Night Journey of Mohammad culminates with his reaching the seventh heaven. Here, enveloped in a golden cloud, he bows before the Throne of Allah in an ecstasy approaching annihilation. The Almighty communicates to him ninety-nine thousand ineffable words of the Law and commandments. (The Pure Land, Taima Mandara, Japan, 18th century. Mohammad's Night Journey, from an illuminated ms., *Mirâj Nâmeh*, East Turkey, 15th century.)

Water, as an element that readily assumes and changes form but ultimately transcends all form, is an apt symbol for consciousness and its transitions. In the heavenly realms, water purifies and nourishes in clear streams and fountains. In the underworld landscapes, it carries the souls of the dead in turbulent rivers or entraps them in foul swamps.

The Egyptian Happy Fields are nourished by the Celestial Nile. Here-Uberkhet, a singer of the sun god, Amen-Ra, is shown kneeling down to drink from the river with the god Geb in the form of a crocodile, suggesting transcendence of the distinction between animals, humans and gods in the world beyond.

An Aztec otherworld landscape shows the dead floating face-down in a swirling river arising from the base of a tree of life. A soulbird stands at one side of the river, a sun temple at the other. (Papyrus of Here-Uberkhet, Egypt, 21st Dynasty. Late Aztec drawing, Mexico.)

In ecstatic mystical states, such as sometimes immediately precede death, it is not unusual to hear music of supernatural beauty; in worship, harmonious sound mediates the worshipper's approach to the Divine.

The vision of St Hildegarde encircles God with nine choirs of angels representing hierarchies of spiritual beings whose harmony reveals His glory. God appears as a disc of brilliant light at the centre: divinity without form. The Hindu god Krishna, incarnation of Vishnu, dances with his beloved Radha in the centre of the adoring circle of gopis or cow-girls, each of whom believes she has Krishna as her partner. The cosmic rhythm of their dance attracts other heavenly beings, who from their airborne ships shower the dancers with flowers. (Miniature from the Breviary of St Hildegarde, German, 12th century. The Dance of Radha and Krishna, Jaipur, India, c. 1750.)

Evidence of funeral ceramics suggests that the Maya had a detailed knowledge concerning the experiences associated with dying comparable to that revealed by the Egyptian and Tibetan *Books of the Dead*. A Mayan ruler of the under-world, wearing a Moan-bird on his headdress, is attended by five women with head-deformations. These were the Chihuateteo, women who died in childbirth and as goddesses lay in wait for children at crossroads to devour them.

In the Chinese and Japanese traditions, the regions of the underworld were governed by a number of Kings of Hell; the four infernal rulers represented here correspond to the four Diamond Kings of Heaven.

Encounters with powerful beings – gods, rulers and judges – des-cribed and depicted in countless visions of the otherworld, have their counterparts in the experiences of the dying and those undergoing symbolic encounters with death.

Such terrifying beings represent the instinctual forces of the human personality. In Buddhist teachings, these beings must be recognized by the deceased as subjective, as they are encountered during the transition period or 'Bardo state' between death and reincarnation. (Drawing after a Mayan funeral vase, Southern Campeche or Northern Peten, Late Classical Period, 600–900, from Coe, *The Maya Scribe and His World*, 1973; Four Kings of Hell, Chinese, Anon.)

Numerous accounts by individuals who have died and then been resuscitated describe vivid and terrifying scenes of judgment. It is as if, at the end of the life-trajectory, the soul reviews and evaluates its own evolution. Often this process is represented as a dramatic 'weighing of souls'.

In a sequence from the Egyptian *Book of the Dead*, the deceased, Hunefer, is brought by Anubis to the Hall of Judgment and approaches the Great Balance. His heart is to be weighed against the feather of truth of the goddess Maat. Below the scale waits Amemet, the Devourer of Souls, a monster who eats the hearts of the unjust. The ibis-headed Thoth records the verdict. On the right, Hunefer has passed the judgment and is led by Horus to be presented to Osiris, lord of the underworld.

A comparable Christian scene shows St Michael before Heaven's Gate bargaining with the Devil for a soul. On the scales the good deeds of the Christian elect are weighed against the evil, while the Devil and his helpers try to tip the balance. An angel raises the judged soul into the hands of St Peter. (Papyrus of Hunefer, Egypt, c. 1350 BC. Altar frontal, San Miguel, Suriguerola, Spain, 13th century.)

Transitions between levels of consciousness are often represented as the crossing of a barrier, such as a door or gate protected by guardians or by magic. The key to the gate may be a magical formula, or knowledge of a secret doctrine. In essence, the key is self-knowledge. The gate of Gehenna, the first of the nine Moslem hells, is approached by Mohammad on his Night Journey. Before the flame-barrier stand the Archangel Gabriel and Malik, Prince of Darkness.

The alchemist who has followed the hermetic river to its source (left) approaches the entrance to the Philosopher's Rose Garden. He must open the locks of the gate with the Twelfth Key of the royal art; that is, he must have attained the appropriate level of esoteric knowledge.

In a scene from the Egyptian *Book of the Dead*, the traveller before the gate is Anhai, priestess and musician of the sun god Amen-Ra. The gates are guarded by gods, half human and half animal in form. (Mohammad's Night Journey, from an illuminated ms., *Mirâj Nâmeh*, East Turkey, 15th century. The Philosopher's Rose Garden, engraving from Michael Maier, *Atalanta Fugiens*, 1617. Papyrus of Anhai, Egypt, 20–21st Dynasty.)

Another barrier to be passed by the soul on the afterlife journey is the river of death, where safe crossing depends on an inner equilibrium. A narrow Bridge of Judgment (above) separates the good souls from the wicked. The souls who succeed in crossing the bridge are directed to Heaven by an angel, while sinners plunge into the river and are carried away to the underworld. From the swamp of the River Styx (right) the damned cry out for aid, or clutch the side of the boat that carries Dante and Virgil in safety through the infernal landscape. In the background burns the hellish city of Dis, and Charon, the ferryman of the dead, makes his rounds. (The Soul crosses over the Narrow Bridge, fresco in the Church of Santa Maria, Loretto Aprutino, Italy, 13th century. Illustration to Dante's *Divine Comedy*. Anon., 15th century.)

The skeletal parts of the body that outlast the flesh are a powerful reminder of death and symbol of the life beyond.

In the Tibetan tantric tradition, death in its dancing form is represented by Citipati: an aspect of Yama, Lord of Death, joined in the yabyam position of sexual union with his female counterpart.

An appliqué of the Cuna Indians of Panama shows a group of skeletons engaged in a lively dance. Though they are symbols of death, they are not terrifying; their basic friendliness is indicated by the little hearts inside their rib cages. So familiarized, the dance of death can be assimilated to the dance of life.

Shamans develop through their symbolic experience of death during initiation the ability to exist in two worlds and travel freely between them. An Eskimo shaman is shown at sunset-time, half red with sunlight and half blue with the shadows of the night. Tradition has it that the shadow aspect can take on independent life and merge with the twilight. At this point, the shaman's body will appear transparent. (Citipati, fresco in the Monastery of Dungkar, Tibet. Appliqué design or *mola* of the Cuna Indians, San Blas Island, Panama. *Shaman*, drawing by William Noah, 1970.)

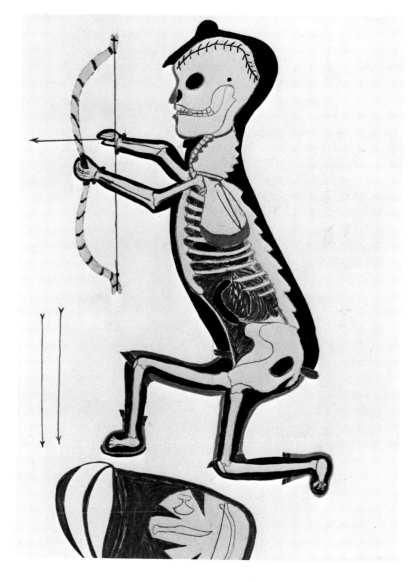

Images of the infernal punishments are strikingly similar even when they spring from very different cultural contexts. It appears that human sins, passions and worldly attachments are projected in forms that are universal. In a Christian image of Hell, the devil spews up the damned on his burning breath, like the biblical monster Leviathan. His helpers fan the flames and torture the condemned souls. In a Buddhist hell-scene, the damned are being tortured by demons in flaming pits. The judgment at the top of the Buddhist hell-scene is the fifth in a series, and takes place at the end of the fifth week in hell. Emma, the Infernal King of this judgment, reaches his verdict after consulting two severed heads, one, red, revealing the evil deeds, the other, white, the good. (Hell, from the Limbourg brothers' *Les Très Riches Heures du Duc de Berry*, France, 15th century. Japanese Hell scroll, 11th–12th century.)

Transition between different experiential realms and aspects of reality is commonly equated with flight, transcending the physical body and the bounds of space and time. The ability to fly between worlds freely and at will is one of the most important powers acquired by shamans during initiation. Birds and animals act as mediators, helpers and soul-guides. An Eskimo shaman is shown carrying his spirit helpers within him – animals and birds who will provide him with food and protection. In the American Indian otherworld, The Happy Hunting Grounds, the dead warriors are shown in flight on magnificent horses. The eagle hovering overhead acts as messenger

between the Land of the Sunset and
the celestial realms. Freya, Nordic
goddess of love and of summer, flies
riding a wild cat and holding a
drinking horn. (*Shaman in Flight*,
drawing by Jessi Oonark, 1971. *The
Sky People*, contemporary Sioux
painting. Freya, medieval painting in
the dome of Schleswig Cathedral,
Germany.)

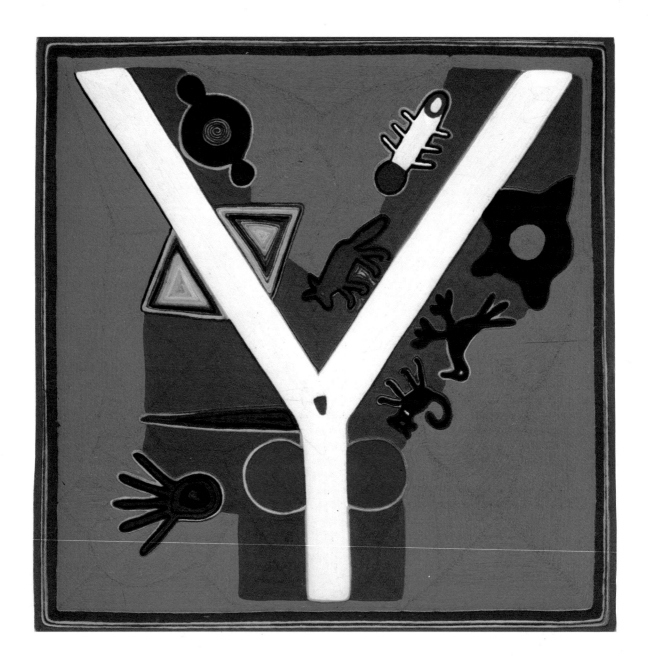

The path to purification and transcendence is through painful ordeals and renunciation. A Huichol Indian map of the Beyond (above) shows a divided path: those with pure hearts take the right-hand path, those with impure hearts go to the left. The ordeals of the left path include impaling on a huge thorn, beatings from people illicitly enjoyed in life, purification by fire, crushing by rocks and drinking of foul, worm-infested water. The soul can then return to the right-hand path, where it must appease a dog and a crow, prove it has not eaten the meat of a sacred animal, and finally, meet a caterpillar, symbol of first sexual experience. Then the soul can complete the journey to rejoin its ancestors.

Another Huichol map (right) shows souls arriving at a wild fig-tree and divesting themselves of the burden of their sexual attachments in the shape of the penises and vaginas of former partners – a concrete image of transcendence of sexuality. In return the souls receive the fruits of immortality. After a feast of figs, maize, beer and peyote, all the souls join to dance around the sun god, Tatevari, 'Our Great Grandfather Fire'.

A painting by a woman who has passed through an experience of an hellish nature during an LSD session (right, below; see also Themes, p. 77) expresses her sense of the spiritual

rebirth that succeeded it. The maternal vagina, which had earlier been perceived as a crushing, murderous instrument, is transformed into a peacock aureole, surrounded by purifying fire and golden light. At the centre of the aureole she is borne up by nurturing hands. (Contemporary Huichol yarn-paintings or *nierikas* by Elijio Carrillo, Central Mexico. LSD painting, collection the authors.)

Purged and purified, the soul approaches union with the Divine. Light, love and joy have become the only realities. In the painting by Hieronymus Bosch (left), the soul reaches the end of the long journey and approaches the Ultimate naked and alone. Dante (above) has passed through the nine circles of Hell, the mountain of Purgatory and the spheres of Heaven; in the company of his beloved Beatrice, he faces the glorious vision of the Empyrean. Here the blessed dwell in a mystical rose, rejoicing in the presence of God. (The Ascent into the Empyrean, by Hieronymus Bosch, c.1450–1516. Vision of the Empyrean, illustration to Dante's *Vision of Paradise* by Gustave Doré, 19th century.)

Gautama Buddha dies, surrounded by all creation – trees, animals, disciples, priests and workers – who are assembled to mourn his passing. He is peacefully leaving the world of sorrow, never to be born again. By his personal example, Buddha has shown mankind the way to spiritual liberation and Nirvana.

The Buddha's 'Four Noble Truths' point the path. According to the Noble Truth of Suffering, emotional and physical pain are intrinsic to existence: birth is suffering, disease is suffering, death is suffering, to be conjoined with things one dislikes is suffering, to be separated from things one likes is suffering. The noble Truth of the Origin of Suffering identifies the cause of suffering as ignorant craving or *tṛṣṇa*: craving for birth, craving for sensual pleasure, craving for death. The Noble Path of the Cessation of Suffering suggests that the pain of living can be transcended by detachment from this craving. Lastly, the Noble Eightfold Path shows the way to cessation of suffering: right view, right-mindedness, right speech, right action, right livelihood, right effort, right mindfulness and right concentration.

This is the Middle Path of the Buddha which gives supreme knowledge and peace, leading to enlightenment and Nirvana. (The Death of Buddha and his Entry into Nirvana, hanging scroll, Japan, 1392.)

Themes

The cycle of death and rebirth was associated in the religion of ancient Egypt with the journey of the sun god across the sky during the day and through the twelve perilous regions of the otherworld during the night. Nut, the sky-goddess, arching to form the vault of the sky, is shown swallowing the solar barge in the evening and giving birth to it in the morning. Its passage through each of the regions of the otherworld, Tuat, is reflected in the successive positions of the sun disc inside the goddess's star-lined body. Beneath the arching Nut await a gallery of gods and demigods whom the Pharaoh is expected to join in death. (Detail of Nut from the tomb of Ramases VI, Thebes, Egypt, 20th Dynasty.)

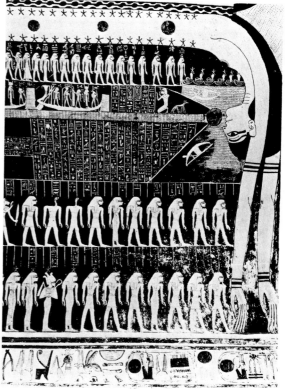

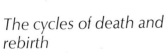

The cycles of death and rebirth

Individuals who transcend the boundaries of ordinary reality and embark on the spiritual journey, typically experience a dramatic change in their concepts of the dimensions of existence. Sometimes they continue to see life as linear, though with an expanded vision of an entire chain of consecutive incarnations instead of the single individual lifespan reaching from conception to biological death. More frequently, the newly revealed fabric of existence consists of cyclical patterns that either return into themselves or follow a helical course. Life thus appears either to originate from its cosmic source, evolve to a culminating point and then dissolve back into the primordial undifferentiated unity, or to proceed along a spiral trajectory, where each return-point represents a higher evolutionary analogue to the one preceding. The cartographies for individual and cosmic cycles of death and rebirth appear in many historical and cultural variants.

Psychedelic subjects frequently experience death and rebirth in vivid sequences comparable to those encountered in the shamanic tradition,

10

11

12

13

14

15

16

17

eschatological mythologies, mystery religions and rites of passage. The artist Harriette Frances, who participated in the LSD programme at Menlo Park, California, documented this process, as it occurred, in a unique series of drawings. After the initial visions of geometrical ornaments (1), the process gradually deepens (2,3) and the artist faces an engulfing whirlpool drawing her into the world of death (4). In the underworld she is subjected to piercing pains (5) and crushing pressures (7). She experiences a strange combination of birth and death (8), meditates on the mysterious symbols on a cruciform altar (9) and is offered assistance (10). In a sequence strongly resembling shamanic initiation, she faces reduction to a skeleton and annihilation (11), followed by renewal, ascent and return to life (12). After what appears to be symbolic crucifixion (13) and reminiscence of some surgical intervention (14), the artist experiences rebirth, associated with the vision of a peacock (15). The following picture of the oceanic womb suggests that the experience of birth opened the way to the unitive state of prenatal consciousness (16). She is returning from her journey with a sense of rejuvenation and revitalization (17). (*LSD Journals of an Artist's Trip*, drawings by Harriette Frances. Courtesy the International Foundation for Advanced Study, Menlo Park, California.)

Cycles (contd.)

The Wheel of Becoming illustrates in a synoptic way the teachings of Tibetan Buddhism regarding the cycles of rebirth. In the centre of the wheel, held in the grip of Yama, the Lord of Death, are three animals representing the 'Three Poisons' or forces that perpetuate rebirth: the pig symbolizing ignorance, the rooster desire, and the serpent aggression. The next circle shows the black descending path and the white ascending path. The six sectors represent the *lokas* or realms into which one can be reborn. From the top, clockwise, these are the realms of gods, titans, hungry ghosts, hell-beings, beasts and humans. In the hellish realm Dharma Raja, the Lord of the Law, judges the dead. On the rim are the symbols of the Twelve Interdependent Causes. (Wheel of transmigration, tanka, Tibet, 19th century. The American Museum of Natural History, New York.)

The theme of death and rebirth is also found in Minoan eschatological mythology. The afterlife is shown here as a progression through four fields created by the boughs of a world-tree or Tree of Life. A pair of lovers is shown during life, and after death reunited in the Land of the Blessed (top left). A sacred lion attended by two hand-maidens is guarding the underworld (top right). The young couple is being ushered into the Hall of the Just, where a griffin with helpers conducts judgment (bottom). (Drawing after the Minoan 'Signet Ring of Nestor', Pylos, Crete, *c.* 1550–1500 BC. From Joseph Campbell, *The Masks of God: Occidental Mythology*, 1964.)

An Australian Aborigine depiction of the soul's journey to reunite with the Eternal Dreaming shows drone-pipe players and dancers (bottom left and top right) performing for the dying man lying on a platform (top left). After death, the man's spirit leaves the platform and begins the long journey to the spirit world. He has to cross over a great snake and kill a fish with a stone for food during his travels. (Contemporary bark-painting by Bunia, Groote Eylandt, Arnhem Land, Australia.)

In pre-Buddhist China, beliefs concerning the afterlife were deeply influenced by a cosmology involving complementary interaction of opposite forces. This is graphically documented on a silken 'flying garment', an ancient funerary robe that was also used as a banner to be carried in front of the coffin during the rite of 'calling home the souls'.

The picture-area can be divided into three main parts; the lower section represents the underworld, the middle the earthly realms, and the upper

section the heavens. The two fish at the bottom symbolize the deepest region of the netherworld, the dark watery abyss of yin, where the souls go after death. The two dragons on the sides represent guides for the two souls of the dead, one yin and the other yang. The little animals on the side waving farewell symbolize the separation of these two souls. The two tortoises with owls on their back stand for the winter constellation of the Dark Warrior, and the ugly man between them is the Spirit of the Northern Seas. On the platform above is a scene with seven men – a rite of divination performed after death.

In the middle section, another ritual scene shows the deceased with three female attendants and two servants offering her food. This is the traditional welcoming-home rite conducted for the dead to assure them of the affection of the family. Below the canopy of Heaven, decorated by two feng-huang birds, the Chinese phoenixes, hovers the Spirit of the East in the form of a bird with a human head. Above the canopy is a gate leading into the palace of the gods, guarded by two leopards and two star-gods, arbiters of human destiny. Above the gate is a bell held by the spirits of wind, sitting on horse-like creatures.

The left upper part shows the crescent moon with a hare and toad, symbols of its waxing and fullness. The woman on the wings of the dragon is Heng-o who became the moon-goddess after having obtained the pearl of immortality. On the right side is the sun disc with a raven; above, the Fu-sang, the tree that the sun climbs and descends during its daily orbit. The juxtaposition of the two celestial bodies symbolizes the return of the two souls to the essence of their being: the yang soul to the sun and the yin soul to the moon. The birds above are messengers announcing their arrival and reunion. The unifying element between them is the legendary ancestor of the human race, Fu-hsi. The ring formed by his serpentine tail symbolizes the reunion of the two souls; divested of all human elements, they are now prepared for a mystical rebirth as ancestor spirits, free of the limitations of time and space. (Silk robe from the tomb of Hsin-Chui, Ma-wang-tui, China, Han period, c. 193–145 BC. Institute of Archaeology, Peking.)

Entering the Beyond

The transition between the material world and the realms of the otherworld can take many different forms. Some belief-systems describe the move from one level to another as a sequence of drastic changes of consciousness. These involve progressive abandonment of the seemingly constant and stable organization of experience characteristic of the phenomenal world and an acceptance of less structured and less predictable modes of consciousness. More frequently, this transition is represented in a concrete way, as entering a cleft in the earth, a hole in the mountains, a volcanic crater or a gate. Although in many cultures such entrances have been associated with specific locations, these references should be regarded, not as geographical, but as symbolic representations of unusual states of mind. The beginning of the spiritual journey is also frequently symbolized by a tunnel, funnel, whirlpool, or gaping mouth of a gigantic monster – Leviathan, dragon, crocodile, whale or tarantula. Most individuals are taken to the otherworld without their choice or even against their will. Exceptionally, gods, demigods or heroes manage to make the journey voluntarily. The Sumerian goddess Inana, the Greek heroes Hercules, Orpheus and Odysseus, King Nimi, the karmic predecessor of Buddha, and accomplished shamans are examples.

In some traditions, supernatural beings assist the souls during their journeys to the Beyond. These beings may be represented as devils and demons, underworld ferrymen, or guides of the dead such as Odin's Amazonian Valkyries of Nordic mythology, or the Greek god Hermes. This function can also be performed by animals or mythological creatures who transport the souls to the otherworld by carrying, escorting or devouring them. Here belong the underworld hounds of the Greeks, Norsemen and Meso-americans, the eagle of the Scythians or of the Greek god Zeus, the horses of the Vikings and Lucans, or Mohammad's mythical mare, Burâq.

On the Lucan tombs the moment of passing away is frequently depicted as a ride on a black horse. The dead are shown as warriors on horseback with sad, absent expressions and limp arms. (Lucan tomb painting, Paestum, Southern Italy, 4th century BC.)

Shamans, too, use animal helpers for their transitions to the realm of the dead. Here a Samoyed shaman rides a bear and plays his ceremonial drum during such a journey. The bear is the animal form of Erlik, the god of the underworld. (Samoyed drawing, Siberia. After Prokofieva.)

It is a common belief among Eskimo and Siberian tribes that shamans can leave their bodies while in a trance and travel to the worlds beyond. The journey into the netherworld is experienced as a descent into the bowels of the earth or the depths of the ocean. A Chukchee shaman dives into the sea to appease the wrath of Anky-Kelé, God of the Ocean. The deity, who is surrounded by seals and whales, has power of life and death over humans, since he controls the supply of animals hunted for food. (Chukchee drawing, Northern Siberia, 1945. After Lavrov.)

A naked young athlete is shown at the moment of his death, which is symbolized by a dive into the waters of the sea. This representation suggests that death is only a transition from this life into the other. (Tomb of the Diver, Paestum, Southern Italy, 480 BC.)

In Greek mythology, the brothers Thanatos and Hypnos, Death and Sleep, assisted the transition between the earthly plane and the otherworld. These two sons of Nyx, Goddess of Night, appeared to mortals when their allotted time was completed. They cut a lock of hair from the deceased as a preparation for Hades and then carried them away

for burial. Here they are seen lifting the body of a warrior from the battlefield of Troy. (Red-figure Greek vase, 5th century BC. Louvre, Paris.)

The journey between the worlds may be assisted by various magical means – direct guidance, prayers, incantations or magic formulae. An Eskimo girl eases her father's passage into the otherworld by 'singing a magic song with magic breath'. With her help he will enter the body of a wolf and eternally hunt the caribou in the Beyond. (*The Dying Man becomes a Wolf*, stonecut/stencil by Myra Kukiiyaut, 1971. The Winnipeg Art Gallery.)

The beginning of the spiritual journey is frequently experienced as being engulfed or swallowed. Thus on a Pre-Columbian sarcophagus, Pacal, the great ruler of the Mayan centre Palenque, falls at the instant of death into the jaws of an underworld monster, just as the sun sinks each day in the west. This image suggest that, like the sun, he will ascend again into the heavens, fulfilling the cosmic cycle. The cross behind the ruler represents the sacred ceiba tree with roots in hell, trunk in life, and branches in the heavens, where a celestial bird perches. (Sarcophagus lid, Pyramid of the Hieroglyphs, Palenque, 683.)

A similar idea is expressed in many medieval paintings and illuminations where the entrance to Hell is depicted as a gaping mouth. (Illumination from the Winchester Psalter, England, c. 1250–60. British Library, London.)

The journey

Like the entrance into the otherworld, the journey through its various regions can be experienced in an abstract way as an unfolding transformation of states of consciousness, or as complicated travel through the landscapes of the Beyond. During the many adventures and ordeals of this passage, the deceased or initiates may rely on their own resources; the descent of some heroes and demigods into the otherworld, or the long walk in the Helshoes described in the Nordic tradition are examples of such independent journeys. In many instances, assistance from divine beings and various means of transportation are available to the traveller. These range from elaborate and magnificent ships and chariots to simple and primitive objects, such as the log that carries the dead Guarayo Indians over the river of the underworld. In many cultures the journey through the Beyond is closely linked to the movements of heavenly bodies, particularly the sun, moon, or Venus, to the diurnal-nocturnal rhythm, seasonal changes or vegetation cycles.

According to many eschatological systems, successful passage through the underworld requires knowledge of its cartography, its specific dangers and the way in which its obstacles may be overcome. Detailed maps developed for the purpose make it possible to prepare for the posthumous journey during life.

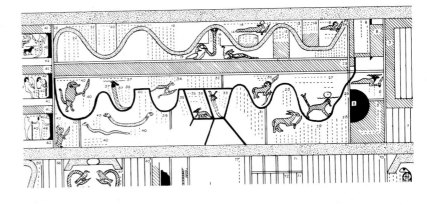

The ancient Egyptian map of Ro-Setau depicts two winding roads: the Road of Water in the upper part of the picture, and the Road of Fire below. During its journey through Ro-Setau, the soul must overcome many obstacles in the form of gates, monsters and evil spirits. After the trials, the soul becomes radiant and pure; it is 'born in eternity' and becomes great and light. Then it is allowed to leave Ro-Setau and enters Anru-tef, the Region of the Happy Ones. (Drawing after a coffin from El Bersha, Egypt, Middle Kingdom. Cairo Museum. From A. de Buck, *The Egyptian Coffin Texts*, VII, © The Oriental Institute, University of Chicago.)

In the Eyptian tradition, initiates and the deceased travel through the otherworld in the solar barge in the company of the sun god Amen-Ra. Here the god is carried to the east by four deities with serpent and scarab heads. (Papyrus of the *Book of the Dead*, Late New Kingdom, Louvre, Paris.)

In Greek mythology, souls were transported across the putrid and stinking underground River Styx in the boat of the infernal ferryman Charon. (Detail, *The Last Judgment* by Michelangelo, 1541. Sistine Chapel, Rome.)

On an Etruscan funeral stele, transport to the otherworld is provided by a chariot drawn by winged horses and guided by a *genius*. (Funeral stele, late 4th to 3rd century BC. Museo Civico Archeologico, Bologna.)

Among the Huichol Indians of Central Mexico experiential journeys into the underworld and contact with supernal realms are mediated by ritual use of peyote. A contemporary image depicting the visionary journey of a Huichol shaman shows him leaving his body, travelling through intricate space-time tunnels of the Beyond, and encountering during his travel spirits of the dead and deities. (Contemporary yarn-painting or *nierika* by Elijio Carrillo, Central Mexico. Collection the authors.)

The image of a boat or a ship in which the souls travel through the nether regions is one of the most common motifs in eschatological mythology. A contemporary version of the Cuna Indian funeral boat shows the souls of people and an animal transported through a colourful world in a craft flying symbolic flags and powered by a Johnson outboard motor. A soulbird in the form of a hawk protects the travellers with its outspread wings. (Appliqué design or *mola* of the Cuna Indians, San Blas Island, Panama.)

The idea of the posthumous journey as a cruise is reflected in a Malanggan ceremony combining commemoration of the dead with ritual initiation of young men. This rite employs carved models of canoes with effigies of ancestral spirits wearing totemic costumes. (Wood carving, northern New Ireland, New Guinea. Linden-Museum, Stuttgart.)

Creatures of darkness

The realms of the underworld are inhabited by hierarchical systems of infernal beings. Their chthonic rulers usually play an important role in the cosmological order, with an authority extending beyond their realms. Through the network of their subordinates they contribute the dark aspect to the phenomenal world, causing disasters, confusion, misfortune and suffering. The polarity between the forces of darkness and the forces of light is sometimes seen as an absolute and *a priori* dichotomy underlying the cosmos. A typical example of this dualistic world-view is Zoroastrianism, in which the entire universe is seen as a titanic battle between the armies of Ahura Mazda and Ahriman. Monistic systems see good and evil as manifestations of the same transcendent creative principle. The best example of this is the Tibetan

Vajrayana, where the same deities have their blissful and wrathful aspects. In the underworld, the infernal rulers and their hosts of subordinate anthropomorphic deities, animals and composite creatures torment the entrapped souls of the deceased and initiates, or subject them to complicated ordeals.

Although the pantheon of the Meso-american cultures cannot be fully reconstructed because of incomplete records, it is clear that the underworld portion of it was unusually rich. In addition to the well-known sources such as the Aztec *Codex Borgia* and the Mayan *Popol Vuh*, much information about Pre-Columbian chthonic myth-ology has been obtained from the study of funeral ceramics. A detail from a Mayan vase shows the underworld god L seated on a jaguar throne. His role as the ruler of the nether regions is indicated by the crossed bones and death-eyes (at upper left), by the strange peccary-like animal with a death collar, above him, and by the vertebrae supporting his throne. (Drawing after the Vase of the Seven Gods, Guatemala Highlands or Northern Peten, Late Classical period, 600–900. From Michael D. Coe, *The Maya Scribe and His World*, 1973.)

Similarly with skeletal shape and insignia, the Pre-Columbian Mictlan-Tecuhtli, Lord of the Dead and cus-todian of the bones of all past human generations, ruled the infernal region Mictlan with his wife Mictlancihuatl. (Totonac ceramic, Tierra Blanca, Veracruz, Mexico, 600–900. Museo de Antropologia de la Univesidad Veracruzana, Jalapa.)

Left-hand page, below:

Visions of devils, demons and other ominous beings similar to those known from eschatological mythology are quite common in psychedelic sessions. They occur typically in the context of the death-rebirth process, when subjects are confronting difficult aspects of their biological birth trauma. A Czech psychiatric patient who painted her vision during one of her sessions labelled it 'It is He', meaning, the Master of Hell. (LSD painting. Collection the authors.)

Fierce and awesome animals populate the underworlds. In one of the hells inspired by the Buddhist sutras, a giant fiery cock sears and mangles those who are guilty of cruelty to animals. (Detail, Japanese Hell scroll, late 12th century. Hara Collection, Tokyo.)

This page:

Among the deities of the Tibetan *Book of the Dead* or *Bardo Thödol* are terrifying goddesses with animal heads who appear on the third day of the Bardo, or intermediate state between death and reincarnation. (Detail, Bardo Mandala, Tibet. Rijksmuseum, Amsterdam.)

Surrealistic monsters with human and animal features express the tearing and devouring tortures of hell. (Detail, *The Last Judgment* by Hieronymus Bosch, c.1450–1516. Alte Pinakothek, Munich.)

Poisonous vipers and constrictors have several characteristics that make them ideal candidates for chthonic creatures. They are closely related to the earth element, represent vital danger, and in shedding their skins, they enact death and rebirth. Aapep, the monstrous serpent-form of Seth, the killer-brother of Osiris, represented one of the major threats of the Egyptian otherworld. As the embodiment of evil and arch-enemy of Osiris and Horus, he had to be confronted by the Pharoah, the deceased and initiates, as he lay coiled in a pit, surrounded by underworld goddesses. (Detail, wall-painting from the tomb of Seti I, Thebes, Egypt, Late New Kingdom.)

The ordeal of hell

The supreme ordeal of the spiritual journey is an experience of physical and emotional agony that seems to be without end. Burning heat and freezing cold, tearing and crushing, torturing sounds, disgusting tastes and noxious smells, combine with feelings of guilt, anguish, despair and humiliation. It is an experience of an insane claustrophobic nightmare.

The soul has to face a strange paradox: in order to be able to continue its journey, it has to accept that it will stay in hell forever. The feeling that the suffering is eternal is an essential experiential attribute of hell. The endlessness of this state does not consist in an extreme extension of linear time, but in its transcendence. The individual undergoes tortures beyond any imagining which at that point are the only available reality; since the sense of the linear flow of time is lost, there appears to be no way out. It is only when this situation is fully accepted that one has experienced hell, and the journey can continue.

In most interpretations of Christianity, the eternity of the infernal state is seen in terms of a period of time of infinite duration. Hinduism, Jainism, Buddhism, the Tibetan Vajrayana and other

Oriental religions consider hells to be temporary stations in the cycle of death and rebirth. In the Mesoamerican religions, hells were not places to which the dead would be consigned for eternal punishment. They were regarded as necessary points of transition in the cycle of creation. It was inevitable that in the cosmic process, all created things should plunge into matter and return to light and their creator.

In a ritual of the Mayan underworld, the infant Jaguar God is about to be decapitated by a young dancing god swinging a knife. A gigantic head of the Cauac monster, a jawless creature associated with rain, serves as a sacrificial altar. The skeletal deity is the death god Cizin; his loin-cloth is decorated with the head of a bone with

death-eyes and the smoke motif, indicating noxious odour. Behind him is the spotted dog who was to carry the dead soul across the river of death on its way to the underworld. The little flying insect with a large cigar is probably the firefly that plays an important part in the Mayan eschatological epic *Popol Vuh*. (Drawing after a Mayan funeral vase from Southern Campeche or Northern Peten, Late Classical Period, 600–900. From Michael D. Coe, *The Maya Scribe and his World*, 1973.)

In the uttermost depths of the Inferno, the triple-headed Satan towers over his victims, devouring simultaneously Judas, Cassius and Brutus. Around him are numerous scenes of ingenious infernal tortures. (Detail, mosaic in the cupola of the Baptistery of San Giovanni, Florence, 13th century.)

  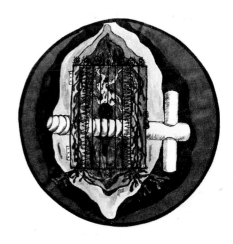

The scene from one of the Buddhist hells shows a prisoner tortured by a demon; the emphasis here is on the element of strangulation and confinement. (Chinese painting, Huan period. Mode Collection.)

The Oriental images of infernal states share many experiential characteristics with their European counterparts. The detail of an Indonesian hell-scene is a particularly poignant representation of the 'no-exit' aspect of infernal suffering. (Painting on linen, Bali, late 19th century. F. Hopp Museum of Eastern Asiatic Arts, Budapest.)

In psychedelic states, the experience of hell is frequently associated with the death-rebirth process. In this context the elements of imprisonment, extreme pressures, excruciating tortures, darkness and fear of extinction seem to be related to important features of biological birth. A painting from an LSD session depicts the vagina as a murderous instrument. (Collection the authors.)

The form of suffering inflicted in hell is not arbitrary; typically, particular ordeals are associated with specific behaviour in one's lifetime. A picture from the Moslem hell shows

Mohammad and Gabriel watching unfortunate sinners who are paying for their hypocrisy, considered a crime of the most extreme gravity. (Illuminated ms., *Mirâj Nâmeh*, East Turkey, 15th century. Bibliothèque Nationale, Paris.)

The experience of being devoured or excreted is frequent in the infernal repertoire, as in psychedelic experience. (Detail, *The Garden of Earthly Delights* by Hieronymus Bosch, c. 1450–1516. Prado, Madrid.)

The universal judgment

The most critical and dramatic phase of the posthumous journey of the soul is the divine judgment. In the paradisiacal and celestial realms the elect enjoy states of pure ecstasy, while in hell the damned are exposed to extreme tortures. The deceased and initiates who undergo judgment are aware of the nature of their potential destinies; their present ordeal consists in their uncertainty of their fate. During the judgment, the life of the individual is reviewed in great detail, prolonging the period of doubt, as good and evil actions are weighed to give the final balance. Usually Divine Judgment is associated with biological dying and death, but it may also accompany symbolic death experienced in psychedelic sessions, the psychotic episodes of schizophrenic patients, or initiation rites. For some religions, the Last Judgment, the final reckoning, takes place with the destruction of the entire world, when all the dead are resurrected and judged together.

The judging principle may appear in abstract form, as a radiant source of light, or, more frequently, with human or animal attributes. Sometimes the souls are judged by means of ordeals such as crossing a treacherous bridge or climbing a ladder stretched between earth and heaven. Only the righteous are able to complete the journey; the sinners lose their balance on the way or are knocked down by demons.

In the Zoroastrian Judgment of the Dead, the deceased have to cross Chinvat Parvatu, or the Bridge of the Separator. To the wicked the bridge presents a sharp edge; haunted by memories of their evil actions, they lose their balance and fall into the abyss of hell. The righteous, for whom the same bridge appears broad and comfortable, pass over it without difficulty and are allowed to enter heaven. (Indian ms., Bibliothèque Nationale, Paris.)

In a Buddhist scene of Divine Judgment, bridges span a pool to connect the upper section with the lower regions. Above is the Paradise of the Supreme

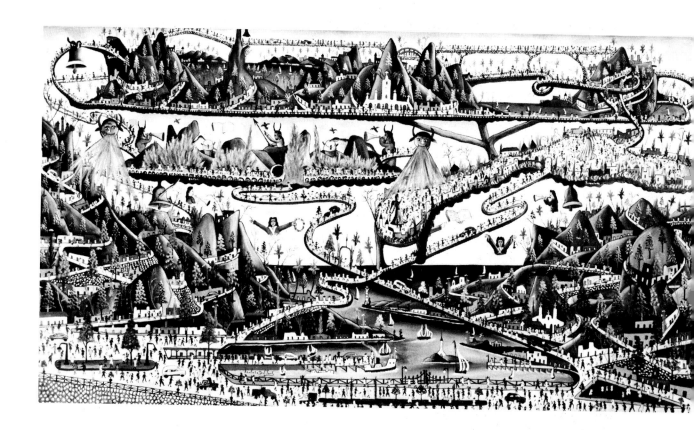

Buddha, populated by radiant beings. Below, seated on his throne, is the Bodhisattva Ksitigarbha, the deity who intercedes with the Judges of Hell. The six figures who float on scarves beside him symbolize his role as the Lord of the Six Conditions of Rebirth. (Scroll painting, Tun-huang, Central Asia, mid-9th century. Musée Guimet, Paris.)

This page:

Haitian imagery combines Christian and African elements. In a scene of Last Judgment that takes place above Jacmel, the devils are shown throwing the damned into the phosphorescent waters of the Carribean Sea. The images of Catholic saints are merged with the voodoo *loa*. (*The Voodoo Vision*, contemporary painting by the Haitian artist Préfète Duffaut.)

On a ladder stretched between earth and the Christian Heaven, those who are burdened by evil actions become easy prey for devils. (St John of Climax, St Catherine's Monastery, Sinai, 7th century.)

79

Judgment (contd.)

Some of the divine judges use instruments to determine the balance of good and evil actions. The scales of justice appear in Christian and ancient Egyptian iconography and in paintings of the Buddhist tradition. Other aids of the divine judges are more culture-specific, such as the karmic mirror of the Tibetan Dharma Raja, or the two tell-tale heads of the Japanese infernal judge Emma.

The Ladder of Salvation is combined here with the scales of justice. (Wall-painting, Church of St Peter and St Paul, Chaldon, Surrey, England, 12th century.)

Osiris, god and king of the Egyptian otherworld, was sometimes represented as the divine judge of the dead. Before his throne stands the Scale of Seven Spirits for the weighing of souls. In the boat, accompanied by two monkeys, is Osiris' evil brother Seth in the form of the 'Pig Destroyer' or 'Devourer of Millions of Years', who swallows those souls that do not pass the judgment. These have to stay in the dark and filthy regions of Amenti and will be exposed to severe tortures. (Drawing after a sarcophagus in the Louvre, Paris. From Wallis Budge, *Osiris and the Egyptian Resurrection*, 1911.)

A Cuna Indian appliqué representing the Last Judgment shows Jesus Christ illumined by the radiant eye of God. In the centre, the hand of St Michael holds the scales while an angel and a devil vie for the souls of the dead. Below are images of heaven and hell, and on either side fly the Cuna soulbirds. (Appliqué design or *mola* of the Cuna Indians, San Blas Island, Panama.)

In a Flemish painting of the Day of Judgment, Christ appears seated on a rainbow, a universal symbol of rebirth and resurrection. With his right hand he blesses the elect as they climb toward the Heavenly Host, and with his left he condemns sinners to damnation. (The Second Coming, from a Flemish Book of Hours, 15th century. British Museum, London.)

The struggle for the soul sometimes takes a mitigated form as an involved disputation between the heavenly forces and the inhabitants of the underworld. (Detail, *The Miracle of Ostia* by Paolo Uccello, 15th century. Palazzio Ducale, Urbino, Italy.)

The uncertain fate of the soul during the Divine Judgment is frequently represented as a physical battle between celestial beings and demonic forces. A Christian version shows the devil snatching the soul that has left the dead body. The Archangel Michael is trying to wrest the soul from the devil while God impartially overlooks the fight. (The Dead Man before God, from the Rohan Book of Hours, France, early 15th century. Bibliothèque Nationale, Paris.)

The Christian theme of 'Abraham's Bosom' is closely related to the Divine Judgment. It suggests that after death but before the Judgment the good souls are raised to Abraham to receive nourishment and protection. Here Abraham holds the souls in a napkin. Two angels accompany the blessed on their journey, while below in the intertwined circle of Hell is the promise of flaming tortures for the damned. (Miniature of the Blessed and the Damned, Psalter of St Louis, France, 13th century. Bibliothèque de l'Arsenal, Paris.)

Left-hand page, below:
According to the Tibetan *Book of the Dead* or *Bardo Thödol*, judgment is experienced during the *Sidpa Bardo*. The judge of the dead, Dharma Raja, is holding in his right hand the sword of discrimination, in his left the karma-revealing mirror. In front of him, the Genius of Good and the Genius of Evil put white and black pebbles on the scale of judgment. The monkey-headed Shinje supervises the weighing, and a jury of animal- and human-headed deities watch the trial. In the foreground, demons are exposing the condemned to various torments. (*The Judgment* by Lharippa-Pempa-Tendup-La, Sikkim, 1919.)

The Chinese tradition has a complex system of hells, each governed by a special ruler with his retinue. One of the ten infernal rulers, Yama, King of the Seventh Hell, is shown here judging the dead. Enthroned, dressed like an emperor, and surrounded by ministers and court officials, he is receiving offerings from supplicants. In front of him, devils with flails and a dog chase condemned souls into a river. (Chinese scroll painting, 19th century. Horniman Museum, London.)

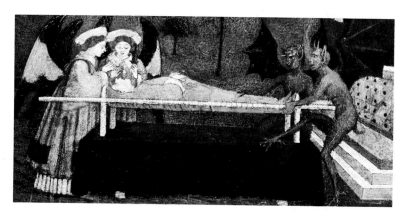

Sound

The experiences of the blessed in the celestial realms and those of the damned in the infernal regions seem to have only one characteristic in common: they involve a sense of transcendence of linear time. There is no access to either past or future, and the divine bliss or hellish tortures appear to be the only existing reality. In all other respects, these two conditions are diametrically opposite. This polarity finds its most immediate expression in the acoustic aspects of these states, since sound and music seem to represent direct manifestations of the cosmic order. Those individuals who have had experiences of the celestial realms tell of the sounds of universal harmony, music of the spheres, nourishing sweetness of divine choirs, and ethereal orchestras resounding with praise of the creator. Conversely, the infernal acoustics abound in dis-harmony and dissonance, creating an atmosphere of chaos, alienation and agony.

Angels dressed in rich garments play trumpets and pluck their lutes. They fill the Christian heaven with divine music, worshipping and exalting the Heavenly Father. (Detail, The Coronation of the Virgin, by Fra Angelico, 15th century. Museum of San Marco, Florence.)

In the paradise of Amitabha Buddha, hosts of celestial musicians play heavenly music amidst radiant clouds. They are Bodhisattvas, enlightened beings who dedicate all the activities of their present and future lives to others. (Detail, Japanese painting of the Heian period, 1033. Phoenix Hall, Kyoto.)

Duality: the extremes of heaven and hell

In the Hell of Shrieking Sounds, described in Japanese Buddhist scriptures, monks who during their lives tortured animals are trapped in torments surrounded by intolerable sounds. (Detail, *Jigoku Zoshi* or Hell scroll, Japan, Kamakura period, *c.* 1200. Seattle Art Museum, Washington.)

In a nightmarish vision of hell, musical instruments become a means of torture, and a knife protrudes from between a pair of ears. Diabolical use of sound seems to add new dimensions of suffering to both the sinners who are freezing in cold hell and those who are being consumed by infernal flames. (Details, *The Garden of Earthly Delights* by Hieronymus Bosch, *c.* 1450–1516. Prado, Madrid.)

Trees and layers

The duality of the paradisiacal and infernal landscapes is well illustrated by the forms and function of their trees. The celestial trees are beautifully shaped and laden with blossoms or exquisite fruit. Their corrupt counterparts are covered with thorns, spikes and daggers, and bear poisonous fruit of disgusting taste, contributing to the suffering of the damned souls.

Sennefer, who during his lifetime was the keeper of the royal parks of Thutmosis III, is shown in the afterlife sitting before the Egyptian Tree of Heaven, whose fruits were believed to give immortality. (Wall-painting from the tomb of Sennefer, Thebes, Egypt, 18th Dynasty.)

A wish-fulfilling tree occupies one of the heavenly realms in the mythology of the Na-khi people of Southwest China. Two levels of gods rest peacefully above the tree, immersed in prayers. Garuda, the golden king of the birds and devourer of evil, sits in its branches eating a serpent. Below right, riding a cow, is King Na-Kaw, ruler of all creatures that have blood. On the left is the moon-coloured horse of foreknowledge who serves as a steed for those who wish to visit the past, the present or the future. From the wish-fulfilling cow near the trunk of the tree comes any drink that one desires, and below her is the white elephant of Indra, king of the gods. (From *The Funeral Ceremony of the Na-khi, Southwest China,* ms. in the Library of Harvard-Yenching Institute, Cambridge, Mass.)

According to the Na-khi tradition, in one of the realms of hell there is a tree made of swords that is rooted in the mouth of Makara, a voracious monster. Two dogs snap at the condemned who are trying to escape by climbing the razor-sharp branches. A demonic couple and ferocious birds represent additional dangers. At the upper right a soul that has completed the ordeal rests on a cloud. (From *The Funeral Ceremony of the Na-khi, Southwest China,* ms. in the Library of Harvard-Yenching Institute, Cambridge, Mass.)

An infernal spike tree was observed in the last of the thirteen sections of hell visited by King Nimi, who is seen in Burma as the fourth incarnation of Buddha Sakyamuni. Several of the damned are forced by demons to climb this tree with its sharp bark and leaves. Those who reach the top are viciously attacked by predator-birds; those who linger in lower parts of the tree are pierced by blade-like falling leaves. (Detail, ms. of the *Nimi-Jataka,* Burma, 1869. Musée Guimet, Paris.)

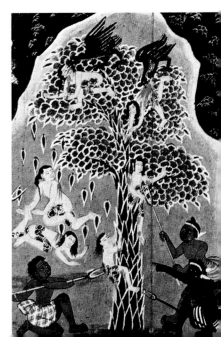

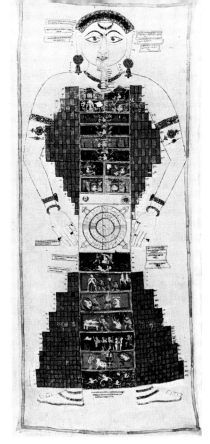

The Purushakara, or Cosmic Man Yantra, a Tantric cosmogram influenced by Jain mythology, shows the macrocosm mirrored in the body of a realized human being. The middle world or earthly plane (*bhurloka*) is represented by concentric rings. The ascending planes of experience are called *lokas* and the descending ones *talas*. The upper region consists of sixteen heavens of sixty-three layers. The lower realm consists of seven earths and forty-nine layers of the subterranean worlds. (Jaina diagram, Rajasthan, India, 18th century. Collection Ajit Mookerjee.)

Below:

A Chinese mythological painting represents the seven sacred mountains, each guarded by a beautiful bird or animal. From the top, these guardians are a peacock, a tiger, a black horse, a white ox, a white mythic lion, the wife of the King of the Birds, Garuda, and a black cuckoo. On the right of each mountain stands a deity, and on the left are a tiger and a bird sitting in the branches of a tree. (From *The Funeral Ceremony of the Na-khi, Southwest China*, ms. in the Library of Harvard-Yenching Institute, Cambridge, Mass.)

In Christian eschatology, Hell is frequently represented as a layered pit. In this vision, influenced by Dante's *Divine Comedy*, a mammoth Devil sits in the middle of Hell squeezing sinners with his hands and crushing them with his claw-like feet. (Hell, engraving after a fresco by Andrea Orcagna in the Camposanto, Pisa, 15th century.)

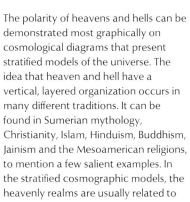

The polarity of heavens and hells can be demonstrated most graphically on cosmological diagrams that present stratified models of the universe. The idea that heaven and hell have a vertical, layered organization occurs in many different traditions. It can be found in Sumerian mythology, Christianity, Islam, Hinduism, Buddhism, Jainism and the Mesoamerican religions, to mention a few salient examples. In the stratified cosmographic models, the heavenly realms are usually related to

the higher regions of the sky. The strata of the underworld or the various hells are located beneath the surface of the earth, and form a layered pit. The earthly realms occupy the middle position between the heavens and hells.

The layered arrangement of the celestial realms is depicted with naive clarity in this Indian painting of the seven floors of heaven, which are superimposed upon the earthly realm. (Miniature, India, 19th century. Bibliothèque Nationale, Paris.)

Emerging

After a deep confrontation with the evil forces and the 'dark night of the soul' comes the glorious turning-point of the spiritual journey. The soul emerges into the radiance of the Divine Light and experiences spiritual rebirth, salvation, redemption, resurrection, reunion. The burden of guilt and fear is magically lifted, evil and aggression suddenly appear insignificant or ephemeral, and the nourishing presence of the divine source becomes the only reality. The preceding agony, loss of faith and alienation seem to contribute to the magnitude of this miraculous event.

This experience of divine epiphany has been described by saints, prophets and hermits in all ages. To some it occurred during intense spiritual practice involving meditation, concentration and austerities. To others it came as an answer to prayers, or quite spontaneously as the grace of God. Similar experiences, of emergence from a dark tunnel or funnel into divine light, have been reported by individuals who have survived clinical death. The phenomena of biological and spiritual rebirth occurring in psychedelic sessions, or the shattering sense of death and transcendence experienced during acute emotional and spiritual crises – seen in Western culture as indications of mental illness – often show deep similarity to this mystical and religious reunion.

Between his death on the cross on Good Friday and his resurrection on Easter morning, Christ descended into Hell, opened its gates and liberated the sinners from their eternal torment. The agony of the Crucifixion freed mankind from the burden of primal sin. A medieval painting shows Christ in front of the mouth of Hell bearing fresh wounds of his martyrdom and haloed in radiant light. The damned, tortured by their separation from God, reverently rejoin the divine element, moving from the darkness of their prison into the light that gives them freedom and immortality. (The Harrowing of Hell, School of Savoy, 15th century. Musée des Beaux-Arts, Chambery.)

The concept of spiritual liberation in the Tibetan Vajrayana is based on a subtle but fundamental philosophical insight. Here, the victory over death is symbolized by the image of Yamantaka, who is the wrathful form of Manjushri and symbolizes wisdom that subdues death. According to the Tibetan Tantric tradition, death is only a transition from a seemingly stable existence to an unstable one. If we truly understand that each moment of our life is the death of the past moment and the birth of the next, we attain liberation and power over death. It is thus essentially our own ignorance that keeps us in bondage. (Yamantaka, Tibet, 17th century. Collection Philip Goldman.)

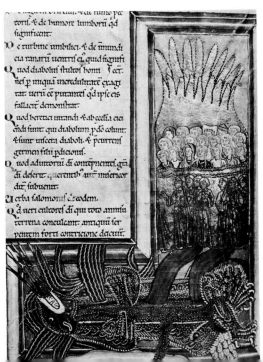

numerous experiences of a blasphemous nature, in which the most sacred elements were contaminated by what she called 'obscene biology'. The patient was able to trace this strange mixture to the memory of her biological birth, a complex experience that combines spirituality with sexuality and brutal physiology. The picture shows the resolution of this problem, as she experienced it at the end of the session. The figure of 'purified Christ' rises in a triumphant way above the realm of 'obscene biology'. However, the patient's hands can be seen reaching toward the Black Sun, symbolizing the Divine without form, the transcendent reality that is even beyond Christ. (Collection the authors.)

Another drawing from LSD therapy shows the patient as a frail foetus surrounded by monstrous predators, symbolizing the awesome power of the uterine contractions. At the same time, the foetus represents the emerging transcendent self, and the monsters stand for the forces destroying the old ego-structures. (Collection the authors.)

A painting by another psychiatric patient depicts an experience of death and rebirth from one of her LSD sessions. Although of a profoundly spiritual nature, this sequence did not involve any explicitly religious symbolism. Her naked body is seen rising in rapture from the realm of death – symbolized by a graveyard, black coffins and a burning candle – with her arms embracing the rising sun. (Collection the authors.)

Left-hand page, below:

For Christianity evil takes a more concrete shape. Since the beginning of time the devil has been the arch-enemy of the divine order and of human souls. In St Hildegarde's vision the beast representing the infernal element is knocked down, chained and rendered harmless by the power of God. The liberation of the souls of the believers was made possible by the self-sacrifice of Christ. The pure religious impulse rises victoriously high above the realm of corruption. (Miniature from the Breviary of St Hildegarde, German, 12th century. Hessische Landesbibliothek, Wiesbaden.)

A similar theme is represented by the scene of an angel rescuing the soul from the purgatorial fire and the grip of devils. According to medieval belief, Purgatory was a place of temporary expiation for the dead who had not entirely satisfied God during Judgment. Unlike Hell, Purgatory allows for hope. After a period of excruciating pain and agony, the soul is purified and qualifies for divine grace. (Purgatory, detail, from Jean Colombe, *Les Très Riches Heures du Jean, Duc de Berry*, France, 15th century. Musée Condé, Chantilly.)

A comparable vision from psychedelic therapy of a psychiatric patient. Earlier in the same LSD session, she had

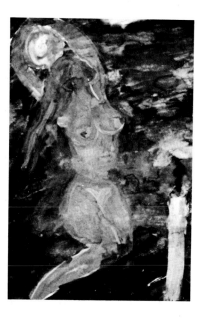

Soulbirds

Universal symbols of the soul, birds appear as spirit-guides, mediators and messengers between the two worlds. In creation myths, the cosmos sometimes originates as a giant egg laid by a creator bird. The peacock is a cross-cultural symbol for the starry heavens and hence resurrection and everlasting life; the swan and the gander play important roles in the mythology of Norsemen, Greeks, Romans and Hindus. Predators such as the eagle, vulture, hawk, kite and thunderbird were closely associated with the deities of the Greeks, Parsees, Egyptians and North American Indians. The legendary Mesoamerican quetzal, the Arabian phoenix and Egyptian bennu-bird symbolize spiritual rebirth and immortality.

Left-hand page:

For the Scythians the eagle symbolized the sky and the solar principle. Here a gigantic eagle carries the liberated soul to paradise. (Scythian gold vessel found in Hungary, 9th century BC. Kunsthistorisches Museum, Vienna.)

The Cuna Indians believe that after death the soul turns into a bird and is taken to the sky-world in a funeral boat decorated with colourful flags. This appliqué shows the soul as a blackbird with rich plumage at the end of its journey to the heavenly realms. A deity sits below, holding flowers and welcoming the novice inhabitant of the otherworld. (Appliqué design or *mola* of the Cuna Indians, San Blas Island, Panama.)

A giant white cock which Mohammad saw on his ride through the first heaven was the angel who was in charge of counting the hours of the day and night. His comb grazed the base of God's throne and his feet rested on the earth. His crow was an act of faith: 'There is no God but Allah!' (Illuminated ms., *Mirâj Nâmeh*, East Turkey, 15th century. Bibliothèque Nationale, Paris.)

In ancient Egypt certain aspects of the soul of the departed were represented as a soulbird. In this scene, the soul in the form of twin birds is seen bowing before the goddess of the sycamore fig. Relatives of the deceased offer sacrifices on his behalf and receive in turn the goddess' blessing – the 'water of the depth' poured down from an ewer. The sap of the sacred sycamore fig was the heavenly elixir of immortality, conferring eternal life on the soul. (Relief, Egypt, 18th Dynasty. Kestner Museum, Hanover.)

The bennu-bird, Egyptian version of the legendary Arabian phoenix, signified the death-rebirth cycle and immortality. It is shown here on a boat with the deceased, Irinefer. The Eye of Horus and solar disc are additional symbols of rebirth. (Detail, wall-painting from the tomb of Irinefer, Thebes, Egypt, 19th–20th Dynasty.)

The ancient Egyptian god-king and ruler of the otherworld, Osiris, personally welcomes his deceased followers after they have successfully passed the judgment in the Hall of Maat. Here Khai and his wife render homage to Osiris before entering the Fields of the Blessed. (Detail, the *Book of the Dead*, from the tomb of Khai and Merit, Thebes, Egypt, Late 18th Dynasty. Egyptian Museum of Turin.)

A comparable scene shows a deceased Etruscan being welcomed to the Beyond by a winged *genius*. (Funerary stele, late 5th to early 4th century BC. Museo Civico Archeologico, Bologna.)

Encounter with Beings of Light

The experience of the Absolute, the Ultimate Reality, transcends all categories and eludes description. It is 'without qualities' and is not bounded by form, space-time, or polar opposites such as good and evil. Paradox and ineffability seem to be inherent to all the accounts of mystical experiences. The Void is the primordial nothingness pregnant with all existence. The Tao that can be described in words is not the Tao. Dharma-Kaya, the Primary Clear Light, that according to the *Bardo Thödol* is seen at the moment of death, has such overwhelming radiance and beauty that the unprepared turn away from it in terror.

Some less extreme transcendental experiences seem to have certain elements that allow for a degree of visualization and empathetic understanding. According to Raymond Moody, many dying people in our culture encounter a 'Being of Light', a source of radiance of supernatural beauty manifesting personal qualities, particularly love, compassion and sense of humour. Often spiritual experiences involve meeting divine beings with quite concrete archetypal features. They can have a distinct form, sexual characteristics, personality, patterns of behaviour, and even specific cultural attributes. Thus many psychedelic subjects have reported religious experiences of a concrete and figurative nature that took the form of encounters with deities of different religions. Individuals pursuing spiritual practices and patients in acute psychotic states have described similar phenomena. Sometimes the visions of these deities are within the cultural framework of the individual; at other times they seem to emerge from the collective unconscious, as described by Carl Gustav Jung. The personages that herald the entrance into the transcendental realms are loving, compassionate and beneficent; they radiate supernatural beauty and have a healing influence on the newcomer.

In the Buddhist temple of Borobudur in Java, a series of reliefs represents the spiritual journey of Sudhana, seeker after the highest wisdom. Pilgrims ascending the graduated stages of the temple can experience initiation by imitating Sudhana in his quest for the ultimate truth. The picture shows Sudhana, who has reached a high point of his spiritual journey, kneeling before Avalokiteshvara, the Bodhisattva of Compassion. (Second Gallery, Borobudur, Java, 18th century.)

According to Eskimo beliefs, the world of the dead is closely related to the Aurora borealis. Here a host of spirits emerges from the dark in the glow of the Northern Lights. In front are dogs which can see the spirits before humans can perceive them. (*Spirits*, contemporary Eskimo print by Pudlo.)

The Australian Aborigines believe that all human spirits travel after death to the mystical island of Bralku. A traditional bark painting shows a new spirit arriving at the island; two spoonbills and two jabirus herald his advent and offer him a ceremonial welcome. (Contemporary painting by the Aboriginal artist Mathama, in the traditional style of the Arnhem Land.)

Valkyries, maidens of the Nordic god Odin, appeared to warriors killed on the battlefield to guide them to Valhöll. The probable interpretation of the scene on this memorial stone is that it represents a warrior's welcome to the afterlife. It shows the dead hero as a rider on Sleipnir, the eight-legged steed of Odin, being met by a Valkyrie holding a horn full of mead. Another of Odin's maidens is hovering above, swinging a spear. The structure on the left represents Valhöll; the ship below symbolizes the journey to the otherworld. (Gravestone from Tjängride, Gotland, Sweden.)

St Peter, who is the traditional Christian guardian of the Gates of Heaven, is seen welcoming the souls of the just. (Detail, The Church Triumphant, School of Giotto, 14th century. Santa Maria Novella, Florence.)

Apsaras, beautiful celestial nymphs of the Hindu and Buddhist pantheons, entertain the newcomers and add to the joy of the heavenly realms with their songs and dancing. (Relief from Angor Wat, Cambodia.)

Paradise

The experience of paradise combines feelings of transcendental happiness and joy with delight in exquisite natural beauty of an earthly quality. The term is derived from the ancient Persian word *pairidaeza*, meaning a royal park or garden surrounded by a circular wall. Although 'paradise' refers to a state of metaphysical ecstasy, it is usually associated with a definite geographical location – a high mountain, large island, or region at the end of the earth. It is separated from the rest of the world by an impassable wall, a barrier of ice, dense and perpetual fog, or a curtain of fire. Inside is a garden of incredible beauty, full of flowers, blossoming trees and tame animals. The air is permeated by exotic perfumes, roads are paved with gold and emeralds, and rivers contain clear water, honey, oil and mead. It is a sanctuary of eternal youth, a place without extremes – an endless springtime that neither winter nor summer can reach.

Although individual cultures and religions show variations in their descriptions of paradise, there are far-reaching correspondences between the Christians and Moslem versions, the Elysian Fields of the ancient Greeks, the Egyptian Happy Fields, the various paradises of Hinduism and Buddhism and the Mesoamerican religions.

A medieval German miniature portrays the Garden of Paradise as a fertile island. God appears as a three-headed figure holding the naked Adam by the hand. The sun and moon overhead symbolize the male and female elements in the universe. (Illustration to *Schwabenspiegel*, 1423. Österreichische Nationalbibliothek, Vienna.)

According to the Taoist tradition, the Eight Immortals have achieved by means of alchemy and yoga the right to feast on the fruit of immortality at the Peach Festival of the Royal Mother Hsi Wang Mu. Here they are seen enjoying eternal life in the Western Paradise of the Goddess. (Chinese scroll painting, 19th century. Private Collection.)

92

The Paradise of the 'Precious Guru' Padmasambhava is a favourite theme in the mystical tradition of the Nyingmapa sect. In this depiction the sacred copper-coloured mountain emerges from the lake, the realm of the Naga king, and rises into the Brahma world. Padmasambhava's celestial palace is translucent from both outside and inside. The Great Guru is enthroned in the centre with two female disciples handing him a Tantric offering. He is surrounded by eight gurus who represent his earlier incarnations. Above his head are the four-armed Avalokiteshvara, Bodhisattva of Compassion, and the Buddha Amitabha. In the sky around the mountain are celestial nymphs, two guardian deities emerging from clouds, and the Buddha Sarvavid-Vairocana. (Tanka, Tibet, 18th century. Swiss Tibetan Refugee Centre.)

The Egyptian Fields of Aaru or Happy Fields represented a way of life resembling the best that earthly existence had to offer. Here the deceased, Anhai, is enjoying a pastoral bliss. She is worshipping gods, cruising the waters of the Celestial Nile, making offerings, tilling the soil and harvesting grain. (Detail from the papyrus of Anhai, Egypt, 20th–21st Dynasty. British Museum, London.)

Chinese mythology refers to a paradise located on the Happy Isles. Its centre is a magnificent mansion, the Palace of Immortality, floating on the surface of the ocean. The three gods of joyful existence crossing the sea are Shou-lao, god of long life, Fu-hsing, god of happiness, and Lu-hsing, god of salaries. They are followed by Hsi Wang Mu, the Royal Mother of the Western Paradise, and her attendant. (From a porcelain dish, China, 1723–5, Victoria and Albert Museum, London.)

93

Heaven and transcendence

For many religions, the celestial realms represent the most desirable goal, the destination of the spiritual journey. For others, they are merely temporary stations in the eternal cycles of death and rebirth, or important but transitional stages in the evolution toward a state that transcends any form of existence. Hinduism, Jainism, various forms of Buddhism, and the Meso-american religions can be mentioned here as important examples of the second concept.

The hierarchical levels and orders of heavens are characterized by progressive disappearance of concrete elements and symbols drawn from ordinary reality. The lower heavens abound in mansions, cities, objects of gold, jewels and resplendent garments. The beauty of the highest realms is of a completely abstract nature. Of all the aspects of the physical world, the heavenly bodies, the star-filled sky and the infinite interstellar space of the far regions of the universe appear to be the only appropriate symbols and metaphors for the experience of the highest heavens. But even descriptions of this kind, that are so frequent in religious scriptures, should not be taken as references to astronomical bodies, three-dimensional space and historical time. The celestial realms represent an experiential reality that does not co-exist with the 'objective reality' of everyday life. Only when the ordinary perception of the material world is transcended – as in deep meditation, psychedelic states, spontaneous mystical experience or physical emergency – can consciousness connect with the heavenly regions. For those who have had the privilege of such experience, the existence of heaven, God and celestial beings ceases to be a matter of belief and becomes self-evident reality.

An example of concrete representation of the heavenly realms, this depiction inspired by Vedic mythology shows the palace of the god Indra and thirty-two smaller mansions. (From *The Funeral Ceremony of the Na-khi, Southwest China*, ms. in the Library of Harvard-Yenching Institute, Cambridge, Mass.)

A comparable Christian representation shows the Celestial City from a bird's-eye view. Each of the twelve gates is decorated with a disc made of a particular gem. The figure of the lamb refers to the words of the Apocalypse (21, 22): '... and I saw no temple therein, for the Lord God and the Lamb are the temple thereof'. (Early medieval Spanish illumination from the Morgan Beatus. Pierpont Morgan Library, New York.)

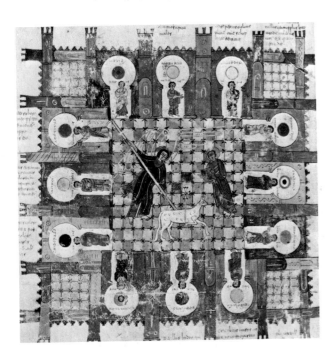

Christian theology describes Heaven as a metaphysical state in which hierarchies of angels and saints enjoy the presence of God and contemplate His being. A medieval illumination shows the heavenly choirs surrounding the Holy Trinity and the Virgin Mary. (The Trinity, from the *Heures d'Etienne Chevalier* by Jean Fouquet, France, 15th century. Musée Condé, Chantilly.)

Dante's vision of the luminous, harmonious Heaven of the Fixed Stars, the ninth of the concentric heavenly realms through which he passes on his spritual journey. (Engraving by Gustave Doré for Dante's *Divine Comedy*, 1861.)

Shiva Maheshvara, representing the essence of all being: the profile on the left side is male, the profile on the right female, while the central face represents the cosmic source that transcends all polarities. (Shiva Temple, Elephanta, India, early 7th century.)

Left-hand page:

The Tavatimsa Heaven is the second-lowest of the six Buddhist heavens of form and sense-perceptions. In one of his previous incarnations the Buddha visited the celestial regions in the form of King Nimi. Here he preaches in Tavatimsa Heaven to the divine beings who join their hands in reverence. (Wall-painting illustrating the *Nimi Jataka*, from Wat Yai Intharam, Chonburi, Thailand, c.1830.)

Bibliography

Budge, E. A. Wallis, *The Book of the Dead*, University Books, New Hyde Park, New York 1960.

Capra, F., *The Tao of Physics*, Shambala, Berkeley, California 1975.

Eliade, M., *Rites and Symbols of Initiation: The Mysteries of Death and Rebirth*, Harper and Row, New York, 1958.

——, *Shamanism: Archaic Techniques of Ecstasy*, Pantheon Books, Bollingen Series, vol. 76, New York, Routledge & Kegan Paul, London 1964.

Evans-Wentz, W. E., *The Tibetan Book of the Dead*, Oxford University Press, London 1957.

Gennep, A. van, *Rites of Passage*. Routledge & Kegan Paul, London, 1960, University of Chicago Press, Chicago 1961.

Grof, S., *Realms of the Human Unconscious: Observations from LSD Research*, E. P. Dutton, New York 1976.

——, and J. Halifax, *The Human Encounter with Death*, E. P. Dutton, New York 1977.

Heim, A., 'Notizen ueber den Tod durch Absturz', *Jahrbuch des Schweizer Alpenklub* 27:327, 1892. (Translation: R. Noyes and R. Kletti, 'The Experience of Dying from Falls', *Omega* 3:45, 1972.)

Huxley, A., *The Doors of Perception* and *Heaven and Hell*, Harper and Row, New York 1963.

Jung, C. G., *Memories, Dreams, Reflections*, Pantheon, New York 1961, Collins, London 1967.

Kuebler-Ross, E., *On Death and Dying*, Collier-Macmillan, London 1969.

——, *Questions and Answers about Dying and Death*, Macmillan, New York 1974.

Moody, R. A., *Life After Life*. Mockingbird Books, Atlanta, Georgia 1975.

——, *Reflections on Life After Life*, Bantam Books, New York 1977.

Noyes, R., 'Dying and Mystical Consciousness', *J. Thanatology* 1:25, 1971.

——, 'The Experience of Dying', *Psychiatry* 35:174, 1972.

Osis, K., *Deathbed Observations by Physicians and Nurses*, Parapsychology Foundation, New York 1961

Rainer, R., *Ars Moriendi: Von der Kunst des heilsames Lebens und Sterbens*. Boehlau Verlag, Koeln-Graz 1957.

Rosen, D., 'Suicide Survivors: A Follow-Up Study of Persons Who Survived Jumping from the Golden Gate and San Francisco-Oakland Bay Bridges', *West J. Med.* 122:289, 1975.

Acknowledgments

The objects shown in the plates, pp. 32–64, are in the following collections: Barcelona, Museo de Bellas Artes de Catalonia 49; Boston, Museum of Fine Arts 39; Cairo, Egyptian Museum 42–43; Chantilly, Musée Condé 56; Cologne, Museum für Ostasiatische Kunst 64; Jaipur, Maharaja Sawai Man Singh II Museum 45; London, British Museum 46–47 below, 48, 51; London, Horniman Museum 57; Madrid, Biblioteca Nacional 33; Mexico City, Museo Nacional de Antropologia 37; Paris, Bibliothèque Nationale 36, 41, 42, below, 50 above; Paris, Musée Guimet 40; Rome, Biblioteca Apostolica Vaticana 53; Venice, Palace of the Doges 62; Wiesbaden, Hessische Landesbibliothek 44; Winnipeg Art Gallery 58.

Photographs and other illustration were made available by the following:

TEXT The authors 28; Edwin Smith 22 below
PLATES Bavaria Verlag 59 below; Eric Cross 59 above; Johannes Fabricus 50 below; Giraudon 56; Sonia Halliday 38; Mansell-Alinari 62; F. Maraini 54; MAS 33, 49; Ann Parker 55 above; Scala 52–53; Sanavik Eskimo Cooperative 55 below, 58; Rodney Todd-White 48, 57; UNESCO and New York Graphic Society 35.
THEMES Alinari 72 bottom r., 76 bottom, 81 centre, 82 top; ATA Stockholm 91 top l.; Peter Clayton 84 top l.; Jean-Marie Drot 79 top; Robert Ebersole 95 bottom; Werner Forman 86 bottom l.; Giraudon 71 centre l., 72 centre r., 86 top, 87 top, 95 top l.; Groningen,

Centrale Fotodienst der Rijksuniversiteit 70 bottom r.; Claus and Liselotte Hansmann 92 bottom: Michael Holford 80 bottom r.; Mansell-Anderson 91 bottom l.; Leonard von Matt 90 centre; National Monuments Record 80 top; New York, Metropolitan Museum of Art 75 bottom; Ann Parker 73 centre l. and r., 80 centre r., 88 top r.; Axel Poignant 68 bottom r.; Princeton University Press 65; Merle Green Robertson 71 bottom l.; Sakamoto Photo Research Laboratory 74 bottom r.; Sanavik Eskimo Cooperative 71 middle r.; Dacre Stubbs 68 bottom l.; Jeff Teesdale 85 top r.; UNESCO and New York Graphic Society 82 bottom, 89 bottom; Verlag St Gabriel 84 top r. and centre r., 85 bottom l., 94 top; Roger Viollet 85 bottom r.; Roger Wood 79 bottom; Elizabeth T. Wray 94 bottom r.